In *Beyond the Darkness*, Clarissa Moll comes alongside all who find themselves in the darkness of grief with a light that points forward toward healing and joy. In these pages readers will find someone who "gets it," someone who has felt the loneliness and the fears that are part of grief, someone who knows what it is like to want the load of grief to lighten while at the same time relishing the way grief helps us to feel close to the person we love who has died. This is a book filled with wisdom and insight that will speak into the questions, the uncertainties, and the opportunities presented to us in the loss of someone we love.

NANCY GUTHRIE, author of *Hearing Jesus Speak into Your Sorrow*

Beyond the Darkness is a gift. It is a guidebook written for all who are confronted with a journey they never wanted to take—the loss of a loved one. In tender prose Clarissa Moll takes our hand and walks with us through the dreadful journey that is grief. She reintroduces us to our loving God, reminding us with awe that God, too, endured the grief of the death of his own Son and yet through that death has removed death's sting forevermore. Add this book to your library. You may not need it now, but when you do, Clarissa Moll will be waiting to walk with you through your grief.

RICH STEARNS, president emeritus of World Vision US and author of *The Hole in Our Gospel* and *Lead like It Matters to God*

Deeply practical and profoundly tender, this is a book that bandages the wounds of the grieving without rushing through the circumstances that put them there. Clarissa's kindness toward her own grief will be a welcome friend to others who mourn, and particularly her insight into how to function through those first hours and days and months. This is a book that can nestle alongside casseroles, gift baskets, and potted plants for the grieving, lingering there still even when the doorstep becomes empty. An unassuming instruction manual for how to make it through the unimaginable.

LORE FERGUSON WILBERT, author of *A Curious Faith: The Questions God Asks, We Ask, and We Wish Someone Would Ask Us* and *Handle with Care: How Jesus Redeems the Power of Touch in Life and Mini*

None of us will avoid an encounter with death—either our own or someone we love. For many of us, that encounter will be what it was to Clarissa: "a mysterious new landscape without a map." Clarissa explored that dark landscape, saw to the light beyond, and brought back to us the map we need. She says this is a book she never wished to write, but thank God she did write it. It is a book that every Christian should read.

WARREN COLE SMITH, president of MinistryWatch.com

Clarissa Moll has earned this wisdom, trudging the hard road of sorrow. I'm grateful she has recorded her steps for the rest of us. She has found there Another walking before her. Reading her brave and luminous book can help you—yes, even you—see him walking with you, too.

JASON BYASSEE, professor at Vancouver School of Theology and longtime contributor to Christian Century magazine

Clarissa Moll is one of my dearest companions, and our grief stories have pulled us closer to Jesus and one another. This book has been fought for and is true and good. *Beyond the Darkness* gives us the hope we desperately need when we can't see a thing, and I'm so thankful she bravely gave us the gift of her words.

MELISSA ZALDIVAR, host of *Cheer Her On* podcast and author

In *Beyond the Darkness*, Clarissa Moll is an insightful and tender guide, a companion who speaks wisdom with gentleness in a place no one chooses to be—a place that is the end of our known world. *Beyond the Darkness* is a balm for the soul, a life raft for those who are drowning. It offers hope and help for the grieving and for those who are walking with them. And it originates from a deep well and provides comfort—especially because it is written by someone who knows of what she speaks. I am deeply grateful for this resource, though it certainly has come at a great cost.

MARLENA GRAVES, author of *The Way Up Is Down: Becoming Yourself by Forgetting Yourself*

Clarissa Moll allows you inside her brilliant mind and tender heart to guide you out of the debilitating pain and suffocating fog of overwhelming grief. I did not want to read about death or sorrow or someone else's pain, but I could not put *Beyond the Darkness* down. I was gripped by the author's raw honesty and deep spiritual insights. Gone are the platitudes and self-help steps you have heard too many times before. This work is filled with the rich wisdom that can only be gained in the house of suffering. Her gentle advice, beautiful prose, and steadfast faith will be a balm to your broken heart.

CHUCK BENTLEY, CEO of Crown Financial Ministries and friend of Rob Moll

Clarissa Moll's book is a beautiful expression of the power of the gospel to bring comfort and hope to those who experience crushing sorrow and unimaginable loss. I have read her book and observed her life. She and her children are members of our congregation who lost a loving husband and a wonderful father in the prime of his life. Most every time I see them, there are tears in my eyes and hope in my heart. Their loss was heartbreaking. Yet their lives are heart mending and hope bringing. All of us experience sorrow and loss. All of us need the hope to which Clarissa's life and book bear eloquent testimony. It is indeed a book of hope, strength, and beauty.

S. DOUGLAS BIRDSALL, honorary chair of the Lausanne Movement

In *Beyond the Darkness*, Clarissa Moll provides a soft place to land for those grappling with the life-altering ramifications of death and grief. Moll combines thoughtful research, tender personal stories, and practical—but not prescriptive—grief support, with a resurrection-centered theology. She invites excruciating pain and stunning hope to coexist in our hearts, our homes, and our communities. *Beyond the Darkness* is a beautiful companion for anyone who finds themself in a season where light seems elusive.

ADRIEL BOOKER, author of *Grace like Scarlett* and the forthcoming *Tethered to Hope*

Clients often wish that their therapist or counselor had gone through the grief journey themselves. Clarissa Moll's *Beyond the Darkness* is a resource born out of personal experience of grief and loss, and she offers a paradigm shift of companionship in grief instead of disenfranchisement from its difficulties. Clarissa's journey in the grief that accompanies her since the death of her husband, Rob, provides an evidence-informed lens for therapists, counselors, and clients in need of sharp and useful tools to survive and thrive in this new path. I highly recommend this resource for any and all who are living and moving in the world alongside grief.

> **REGINA CHOW TRAMMEL, PHD, LCSW,** associate professor of social work at Azusa Pacific University, licensed psychotherapist, and coauthor of *A Counselor's Guide to Christian Mindfulness: Engaging the Mind, Body & Soul in Biblical Practices & Therapies*

In *Beyond the Darkness*, Clarissa Moll offers tremendous wisdom and hope, even as she candidly explores the many layers of loss. A wise and tender guide, Moll bravely invites us into a journey through the shadows of grief—and into the healing balm of companionship.

> **DR. ALISON COOK,** counselor and author of *Boundaries for Your Soul*

As a sudden and unexpected widow myself, I resonate with all Clarissa has to say in her insightful book. She writes beautifully, observes carefully, and translates a dark passage of life into language we can understand and benefit from. As she courageously notes in her book's title—*Beyond the Darkness*—we do indeed come out the other side of darkness, death, and grief into light, life, and resurrection. I am so glad for that truth and thankful that Clarissa is pointing the way forward.

> **CAROL L. POWERS, JD,** cofounder and chair of the Community Ethics Committee, Harvard Medical School Center for Bioethics

CLARISSA MOLL

BEYOND

A Gentle Guide
for Living with Grief
& Thriving after Loss

THE

DARKNESS

TYNDALE
MOMENTUM®

A Tyndale nonfiction imprint

Visit Tyndale online at tyndale.com.

Visit Tyndale Momentum online at tyndalemomentum.com.

Tyndale, Tyndale's quill logo, *Tyndale Momentum*, and the Tyndale Momentum logo are registered trademarks of Tyndale House Ministries. Tyndale Momentum is a nonfiction imprint of Tyndale House Publishers, Carol Stream, Illinois.

Beyond the Darkness: A Gentle Guide for Living with Grief and Thriving after Loss

Designed by Dean H. Renninger

Edited by Jonathan Schindler

Published in association with the literary agency of Wolgemuth & Associates.

For information about special discounts for bulk purchases, please contact Tyndale House Publishers at csresponse@tyndale.com, or call 1-855-277-9400.

Library of Congress Cataloging-in-Publication Data

A catalog record for this book is available from the Library of Congress.

ISBN 978-1-4964-5893-3

Printed in the United States of America

28 27 26 25 24 23 22
7   6   5   4   3   2   1

To K. N. J., who held my hands

"*Come, Mr. Frodo!*" *he cried.*

"*I can't carry it for you, but I can carry you.*"

J. R. R. TOLKIEN, *THE RETURN OF THE KING*

To my beloved children

that you may know him and the power of his resurrection,

having been acquainted with his sufferings

CONTENTS

INTRODUCTION

It is comforting to think that our tears are put in a bottle and not one of them forgotten by the one who leads us in paths of sorrow.

HANNAH HURNARD, *HINDS' FEET ON HIGH PLACES*

Dear reader, this is a book I never wished to write about a life I never wished to live. When my husband, Rob, died three years ago in a tragic hiking accident at age forty-one, I found myself dropped into a mysterious new landscape without a map. I was bewildered and frightened, a young widow with four children. I could see no trails stretching before me, pointing the way. I felt entirely lost in grief.

I suspect if you hold this book in your hands, you share a similar sorrow. This is a book you never wished to read for a life you never wished to live. You have lost someone dear to you. Whether death has surprised you or you've seen it coming, grief has brought you to your knees and threatens to undo you. You struggle to keep your head above water as wave after wave of sorrow breaks over you. You feel lost, alone, isolated, unheard, abandoned in a dark forest of suffering. I want you to know that I understand. The particulars of your sorrow are in your precious keeping. But the landscape of grief? I know this well.

Perhaps instead, you're walking beside someone dear as they discover the strange topography of death and grief. You've committed to holding space, to remaining in the face of a specter that causes others to flee. Yours is a courageous task. Your wisdom, constancy, patience, and kindness will be called upon in this season in ways you never could have imagined. You will be a living gift in the face of death.

Maybe grief feels painfully familiar. You've lived with it for a long time now. Years after your loved one's death, you carry a deep pain that seems little changed from those first days of shock or sorrow. You wonder, after so long, *How could it possibly still hurt so much?*

In one way or another, death has drawn near to you. Its nearness has made you willing to look at something we usually avoid at all costs. For many of us, our unwillingness to sit with death has made us woefully unprepared to face it. But regardless of your preparation for this moment, you're here now. Life calls you to walk with grief. There is no need for regret, for wishing you'd paid attention before. Now is the time for love and grace, for finding a way forward in the midst of suffering. Would you walk with me? Let's take this hard journey together.

It is not lost on me that this book exists precisely because my husband died. For all my satisfaction in completing a project such as this, I'd give it all up in a moment to have Rob back with me. His death has left deep scars on the landscape of my life, and I miss him every day. But on this journey of grief, I have also discovered grace. I have learned core things about who

I am, about who God is, about what Jesus offers me. I have learned, though much afraid, that I am never alone. My Good Shepherd walks beside me. These, too, are gifts I would never wish to give up. I believe they are available to you, too.

Those who grieve are often reminded that "the LORD is close to the brokenhearted." But what does that look like when we are lost in the darkness of agonizing sorrow? How do we train our ears to listen for the soft trickle of that Eternal Spring in a dry and weary land? How can we find grace in the grief that has befallen us? When we can't trace God's hand, how can we ever find a path forward?

For the Christian, Jesus' presence in our grief changes everything. I cannot promise you that his presence will make the pain hurt less or the healing come more quickly. I cannot promise you that, this side of glory, you will ever understand why this sorrow has shadowed your path. But I can assure you that the companionship of a Savior who bears scars is the thing grieving people need more than anything else. In Jesus we find the Friend who understands.

Dear reader, I know that you want to know when this hurt will end. When the searing ache of loss will ease away. When you will find yourself again. I wish I had easy answers. In my days of loss, I've desperately hunted for them myself. Each time, I've come up empty-handed. Instead, at the end of all my searches, I have found these two truths always standing clearly in my path: Grief will walk with us all of our earthly days. Our Savior will too.

At its core, this book is about these two truths. Grief, this unwelcome companion, will accompany you on your life's journey. She has filled her satchel with tears—her food day and night—and she will walk beside you. She will travel with you through the valley of the shadow of death. She will join you on the mountaintops of joy. Her presence will ever remind you of all that remains broken and sorrowful in this fallen world. If you're to walk with her, I believe it behooves you to know her well.

But do not fear. The path is wide enough for another companion, the Good Shepherd of your soul. The Compassionate One whose gentle hands bear the scars of death. The beautiful Resurrected One who has been there and back again. In your darkest hours on this path of sorrow, Jesus will be present. When the landscape is made barren by grief and filled only with painful silence, the Spirit will intercede for you with words that cannot be expressed. When the path of sorrow grows treacherous, the almighty Father will carry you with strength and tenderness. In his merciful goodness, he will teach you to sing, "I fear no foe, with Thee at hand to bless."

In the following pages, you'll find practical ways to engage with grief, to meet—perhaps even befriend—this unwelcome companion. You'll uncover the lies the world has told you about your grief, and you'll meet her face-to-face, as she really is. With honesty and compassion, you will learn to turn *toward* grief instead of pushing her away. You'll learn to navigate your new life with grief as your companion, taking her places you never thought you could.

And as you do this hard yet necessary work, I hope you will discover Jesus on your path of suffering. It is my prayer that the light of his presence would direct your feet as you take these next steps in grief. That your sorrowing body would find repair in his gentle embrace. That your wounded spirit would be made strong by his enlivening Spirit. That your soul would find the refreshment of his living water in the parched places of your life.

CHAPTER 1

On the Path with Sorrow and Suffering: The Journey Nobody Wants to Take

"They are good teachers; indeed, I have few better. . . . This,"
said [the Shepherd], motioning toward the first of the silent figures,
"is Sorrow. And the other is her twin sister, Suffering."

HANNAH HURNARD, *HINDS' FEET ON HIGH PLACES*

When the police chaplains arrived at my campsite, I told them I needed them to wait until I had someone to hold my hands. I told them I couldn't hear their words until I wasn't alone. I told them they would have to say what they needed to say in a single sentence. One sentence that would somehow tell it all. Their allotted airtime. Their character limit. I knew the news was bad. I knew how little I could bear in that moment.

"Your husband was in a hiking accident today, and he fell to his death."

Did the chaplain say Rob's name? Was it one sentence or

two? How could a single sentence be the sum? I still parse the moment in my mind, searching for language to express the darkness that overtook my life as he spoke. I have more words now to explain the details of my husband's accident. That night remains as vivid as the night Rob and I met. Yet even three years later, I struggle to describe the weight of Rob's absence, my life without him here. The thought of losing him still takes my breath away. The grief still runs so deep.

Before the chaplains left that night, after they had repeated their sentence to my four young children, we stood outside together in the summer night. "I need to say the words," I told them. And so I repeated that single sentence, made it real by saying it aloud. Like God the Father at the dawn of creation, I spoke Rob's death into existence for myself. Not like the muddled mumbling of the dream-addled mind in sleep. But clear, simple, shaking, afraid, real. I stood in the twilight at my campsite, three thousand miles from home, and I listened as my own voice spoke the truth with which my heart will always wrestle. My precious husband was dead.

STANDING AT THE TRAILHEAD

One early morning, on our family vacation, my husband Rob left our campsite for a long hike in the backcountry of Mount Rainier National Park. Rob and his hiking partner set out on the trail that day excited and energized for the path ahead. Both loved hiking and knew how to do it well. Being in the wilderness was Rob's favorite way to recreate and connect with God. But his body returned to the trailhead late that afternoon, airlifted by a helicopter out of the wilderness, cold and lifeless.

This day, marked on the calendar as a highlight of our family trip, became the most sorrowful of our lives.

In a moment, my world changed forever. I am still dumbfounded at the swiftness of death's destructive work. Rob's death ushered me into a harsh, lonely landscape of loss. His sudden tragic passing erased my plans for the future and set my feet at the trailhead of a new, unwanted path. For the rest of my days, I would walk with grief. I would travel down a trail nobody wants to take.

I never knew deep grief until I lost Rob. I had suffered other losses but none that broke me so profoundly, none that rearranged the entire order of my life. I will admit, from the very beginning, I have been a reluctant traveler on this new path of sorrow. Left with four children to raise alone, there is not a moment I do not long for the life I lived before. Rob and I enjoyed seventeen imperfectly wonderful years of marriage. Our life together was deeply satisfying. We shared the same passions and dreams. He loved me with all his heart, and I adored him.

As Sorrow and Suffering have beckoned me forward onto this grief journey, like Much-Afraid in Hannah Hurnard's classic *Hinds' Feet on High Places*, I have cried out to Jesus, "I can't go with them. . . . I can't! I can't! O my Lord Shepherd, why do you do this to me? How can I travel in their company? It is more than I can bear."

And yet, here I am. I have survived the moment I thought would be the death of me, too. I walk a trail of sorrow I never imagined I could. I have come to embrace grief as my companion, even if every day I long for her departure. I live in the valley of the shadow of Rob's death, and yet I also choose to lift my eyes beyond this daily darkness toward horizons that promise flourishing. I have vowed to myself, "I shall not die, but live, and declare the works of the LORD." And I believe you can do these same things too.

WHAT HE LEFT BEHIND

The list grows long when I consider the things Rob left behind when he died. Rob left friends, colleagues, and a job in which he found purpose. He left parents and siblings and an extended family who loved him very much. He left our children and me, alone now to forge a path forward without him.

Rob's tragic death ended his life in its prime and brought death to our family in its blossoming years. Never again would our sons enjoy Dad as coach for Little League. Never again would his voice rise in a hearty cheer above the crowd at a 4-H competition or dance recital. Our dreams of retirement and empty-nesting would never come to be.

When I returned home from his memorial services that summer, from our road trip that had ended in grief, I discovered a little bar of Irish Spring soap on the shelf in my shower. We'd left it behind when we packed for the road. It was too small to be worth bringing along. Rob never returned to use it again. Even his soap he'd left behind.

These losses do not tell the whole story, however, for Rob also left behind a legacy of words. A journalist and author, Rob made his career in writing. He wrote about business and faith, humanitarian aid and finance. And, in what has become an unexpected, exquisite gift to you and me, he wrote about dying.

Early in our marriage, Rob wrote a book called *The Art*

of Dying. His journalistic curiosity and deep faith led him to work in a funeral home. He joined a hospice organization and became a volunteer, visiting with terminally ill patients on the weekends.

In the course of writing *The Art of Dying*, Rob discovered that for the last two hundred years, dying had shifted out of public view. In recent years, most people died in nursing homes or hospitals behind closed doors. Few families, communities, and churches attended well to dying people. Few people prepared for death—their own or those they loved. For most, until they experienced the death of a close friend or family member, on-screen deaths in movies and video games—broken down into pixels and distanced by the ability to hit the off button—were the only ones they knew.

As Rob worked his shifts at the funeral home, he saw that those who grieved had similarly poor preparation. Because death was pushed into the shadows, grief was too. Nobody knew what to do, so few people did anything at all. Employers asked bereaved workers to return quickly to the job, and communities and churches continued their programming and services as usual. Rob saw hurting people regularly encouraged to pull themselves together and move on. He saw dying and grieving people struggle in a culture that simply didn't understand.

IS IT POSSIBLE TO GRIEVE WELL?

Rob's writing about death profoundly shaped our early marriage. I edited *The Art of Dying*, and over many nights through the years, Rob and I talked about dying. We discussed our end-of-life choices even though we were young; we outlined our desires and knew each other's wishes. We compiled our end-of-life documents and bought life insurance. We were committed to being a death-literate couple.

Knowing this, many people have asked me if I was prepared for Rob's death. I always tell them yes and no. Even though his death came as a surprise, I knew what he wanted. When Rob died, I simply executed our conversations to the best of my ability. Yes, I was prepared.

And yet, there is nothing that can prepare you for the agonizing loss of a loved one. You can read a biography of Rachmaninoff and listen to hours of his symphony recordings. You can sit in scholarly seminars and engage in discussions of his works. You can know everything there is to know about his music. But as you sit before the piano, your fingers lightly settled on the keys, you find you cannot play a single note of his Piano Concerto no. 2. Not even a bar. With all your knowledge, your fingers, your brain, and your heart do not know the score. To play, you must learn the notes. And the only way to learn is to practice—in real life.

As believers, we can face death and grieve with full confidence. Our lives are in the strong and tender grip of our Good Shepherd. Grief may walk with us our whole lives, but our Savior does too.

This is how I have found my grief journey to be. Picking through the weeds, bushwhacking through the forest, hunting for signs I was headed in the right direction. Trying to learn this new terrain of sorrow. Grief has been a painful education; I have had to learn as I go, fumbling and trembling along the way. I do not write as an adviser but as a fellow pilgrim, sharing what I've learned on this path of sorrow, offering you companionship.

From what I have seen, I believe you can acquire the skills to grieve well. While each loss is unique, I don't believe we need to stumble blindly along the path of sorrow. Grief brings deep darkness, but we can learn how to navigate it in ways that make our pain more bearable. As believers, we can face death and grieve with full confidence. Our lives are in the strong and tender grip of our Good Shepherd. Grief may walk with us our whole lives, but our Savior does too. Indeed, as we walk together through the valley of the shadow, he calls us beyond the darkness to resurrection hope.

SAYING THE D-WORD

Every Thursday, our smell announced our arrival before we hit the threshold of her classroom. Teenage boys tumbled out of the locker room, doused in cologne to mask their gym class body odor. Girls walked down the hall in groups, a cloud of floral shampoo fragrance surrounding them.

"Women don't sweat; they glow," my high school English teacher would remark as we filed through the door and headed to our seats. An agreeable sentiment—unless you had to wear medicated deodorant. For at least one girl I knew, those words were laughable. Adolescence had hit her like a Mack truck. Women didn't just sweat. They stank. No euphemism was adequate when the medical community had to assist you in taming your odor.

Death is the ultimate stink. We've got all kinds of genteel phrases to try to mask its horrid smell. Our pets *cross the rainbow bridge.* Our loved ones *pass away* or *go to a better place.* Become a Christian, and the phrases multiply a hundredfold. *Gone to be with the Lord. Crossed the river Jordan. Entered eternal rest. At peace with God. In the arms of Jesus. Called home.* All phrases that help us avoid saying the word we really mean—*died.*

In grief, I have clung to Jesus and to the promises I find in God's Word. To be absent from the body is to be present with the Lord. Those who have died in Christ now enjoy his promised eternal life. Jesus has prepared a home for those who love him. These promises form the bedrock of my hope.

But in a society that already doesn't know how to talk about death, these promises can easily just become euphemisms—attempts to deodorize death, take the edge off its horrid smell. They can even distract us from grieving well. That's why I'm committed to using real words about death and grief. As your first step toward grieving well, you can do it too.

You have sat at the bedside of a loved one. You have received the dreaded call in the night. The police chaplain has visited you like he visited me. You have met with Death. You know it is futile to dress up that word. *Dying. Died. Death. Dead.* We do not say these words to shock others. We use the d-word because death is real and our sorrow over it is worthy of acknowledgment. We do this because before he raised him from the dead, Jesus stood at Lazarus's grave and wept. No euphemism can soften the blow. Death hurts. Period.

A COMPANION IN SORROW

Have you discovered the painful truth that few in your life can understand your loss? Do you stand at the trailhead of your grief journey alone? Have you realized you cannot depend on your community or church to support you in the slow work of rebuilding your life? If so, you're less alone than you think. I'm here with you.

The purpose of this book is to fill that gap, to offer you a companion on your path with grief. There is a special kinship with those who mourn, and I hope you find it in these pages. No one can understand your unique loss, but those who grieve recognize the range of emotions, the painful firsts, the hole that loss has bored into your heart and life. These things are universal to grief and therefore ties that can bind our sorrowing hearts.

In these pages, I offer myself as your companion in sorrow. Not only do I hope you feel less alone as you read this book, but I hope you find practical help and support from a fellow traveler on this path. Grief can make us feel like the world no longer understands us. If we're honest, we hardly understand ourselves anymore. Old friendships and even family relationships grow thin, and we wonder if the death of our loved one is a death for us, too. I understand one hundred percent. However, this path is more traveled than you think; there is companionship to be found here.

This book has a second purpose: to acknowledge the long-lasting, pervasive nature of grief. It's time for a paradigm shift in how we talk about bereavement. Because our culture doesn't want to look at death, we hope people will "wrap it up quickly." But grief lasts a lifetime. This world is a hurting, broken place, and even in the midst of resurrection hope, sorrow still exists. Grief, like love, lives on long after death. Until Jesus comes again, grief will walk with us. It is only when we acknowledge this lasting nature of grief that we can learn to live with it as our companion and look for a life beyond the shadows of our sorrow.

This book's final purpose is flourishing, plain and simple. Many times since Rob died, I have had to remind myself that I have not died too. Parts of me are gone forever, yes. But blood still courses through my veins. My heart beats a steady rhythm. I am still alive. And I do not merely want to "hang on" for the rest of my earthly days. I want to live them fully, in the same wholehearted way I did before death and grief darkened my doorstep. I want the pain of Rob's death to transform me, not cripple me.

We can discover flourishing not in recovery from grief but in companionship with it. In our weakness, God's strength transforms us. Little resurrections are possible for us every day as we await the grand fulfillment of God's promises in Jesus Christ.

Flourishing after the death of a loved one is a choice we each must make. We must choose to move in that direction, to pursue new purpose and growth. But as people rooted in resurrection hope, we believe new life always is straining to grow up out of the soil of death. Like autumn flower bulbs in paper bags awaiting sunny warmth, we too are waiting to bloom from the darkness of grief.

New life after loss isn't pie-in-the-sky hopefulness. It is the product of our willingness to sit with our grief, to allow it to take up residence as a thorn in the flesh that will persistently sting us until all things are made new. We can discover flourishing not in recovery from grief but in companionship with it. In our weakness, God's strength transforms us. Little resurrections are possible for us every day as we await the grand fulfillment of God's promises in Jesus Christ. You can live a full and joyful life in the face of death. You can survive and thrive holding hands with both grief and God.

HOW TO USE THIS BOOK

This book is organized into three distinct parts, though I acknowledge grief resists categorization. I've structured it this way so that you can hop onto the trail anywhere you need.

Any long journey requires preparation, and the path of sorrow is no different. Before they ever hit the trail, experienced hikers spend hours poring over maps, discerning elevation, and looking for potential pitfalls. They identify spots for rest and sources of water. Part 1 offers you a similar kind of orientation. As you begin your grief journey, I will help you identify roadblocks, pitfalls, and dangers on the path that lies before you. You will learn the boundaries of the trail and hidden sources of nourishment. Most of all, you will take the time to meet and listen to your new companion, grief. If you find yourself dismayed by grief or by your family's or friends' response to it, I encourage you to start here. I think you'll find some helpful guidance for orienting yourself to your sorrow.

Once hikers have their trail mapped out, it's time to assemble their gear. Travelers into the backcountry regularly pack "ten essentials." These are their survival items like a map, compass, and fire starter. You'll find part 2 is full of survival essentials, practical insights for those of us who have acknowledged grief as our companion. If you are up to your neck in acute grief, skip right to here. You'll feel heard and known in these chapters, and you'll gather tools to help you keep going when it feels like the trail is too dark to see. You will become equipped to survive the hardest stretches of your journey with sorrow and suffering.

Finally, as time passes after our loved one's death, many of us discover that the journey of grief appears to have no end. Fatigue and discouragement can set in. You might question whether life can shine again brightly with hope like it did before your loss. Part 3 acknowledges the continuing nature of our grief and casts a vision for a Christian community that supports the long-term needs of the bereaved. If you are further along in your grief journey, you may want to start here. Part 3 will offer you inspiration as you see your grief placed in the context of a faith community and in the light of gospel hope. Infused by the Spirit's comfort and power, you can do this hard thing.

THE SOAP HE LEFT BEHIND

Do you remember that little bit of Irish Spring soap I told you Rob left behind? When I first realized this was his last bar of soap, I treated it like a museum artifact. I carefully moved the little nub out of the water's spray and placed it on a shelf in the shower where it rested beside his razor. It was just a scrap, really. But I didn't have the heart to use it; it had been in my shower since before he died. That soap felt so intimate: his body was the last it cleaned.

That little bit of soap held all my fears in it. I feared the waters of sorrow wearing me away into something small. I feared that with time my life would change shape so dramatically that no trace of Rob would be left behind. I feared the using up, the replacing with something new. Preserve or use up. It's all-or-nothing thinking, I know. Fear does that to my heart and mind.

But then I remembered there's a third way. (Isn't there always, if we look for it?) When I was a girl, my mother used to take the diminishing soap bar in the shower and place it atop a new bar—an attempt to waste nothing, no doubt a Depression-era trick she'd learned from her mother. The two bars sat against each other when wet, and as they dried, the two would harden into one. The two soaps developed a strong bond, unable to be separated, even with the wearing down of subsequent use.

Inspired by that long-ago memory, I placed Rob's little soap atop a new one in my shower. His old, small Irish Spring now rested against my new lavender bar—a picture of my grief for his death bonded forever with the new life I'll live without him.

My soap bonding isn't just a sentimental ritual. It's a picture of the way we can live our lives in the face of loss. We can find new life, bonded forever with those we have loved, even as we must face the slow fade of their lives from ours. Our lives, stronger, because they connected so deeply to those we have lost.

Life—like soap—is made for using, not for saving. Our lives, though marred by sorrow and colored by grief, are made for flourishing, not death. We were made for use, for work and prayer and praise, not in isolation from grief but in the midst of it. In the hands of the Good Shepherd, pain can be transformed into purpose, life redeemed from the pit of despair. Even our grief need not be wasted.

On her own journey to the High Places, little Much-Afraid finally consented to her new companions, Sorrow and Suffering.

She mused, "Others have gone this way before me . . . and they could even sing about it afterwards." The Shepherd promised Much-Afraid that her companions would take her where she needed to go. Grief would be her guide on the path to the High Places. As we walk together, I trust the same will be true for you. Let's point our feet forward, then, to the path before us.

FOR YOUR OWN REFLECTION

1. Before your loved one died, what experiences did you have with death?

2. What cultural practices have made it hard for you to acknowledge your loss?

3. Can grieving begin before a person's death? If so, how could that be helpful?

4. Have you talked with your loved ones about your own death? Why or why not?

5. How does it make you feel to hear the phrase "Grief is your companion"?

PART 1

PREPARATION

FOR THE

JOURNEY

CHAPTER 2

Obstacles on the Path:
Four Myths We Believe about
Grief and Loss

*Believe me, when you get to the places which you dread you will find that
they are as different as possible from what you have imagined.*
HANNAH HURNARD, *HINDS' FEET ON HIGH PLACES*

In high school, I toured in a reader's theater production about five missionaries who were martyred in the jungles of Ecuador in 1956—Jim Elliot, Nate Saint, Roger Youderian, Ed McCully, and Pete Fleming. Their deaths made international news and ignited North American missionary enthusiasm in the twentieth century. As a teenager, I read Jim Elliot's published journals and devoured the stories of his life written by his wife, Elisabeth Elliot, after his death. Something about their story struck a chord within my heart.

Each night, I performed as Elisabeth, the lead character, a gutsy young mother and wife. Over the course of ninety minutes, I became a widow in every performance. I remember discussing missionary plans with Jim and later urgently trying to make radio contact with him from the Shell Mera station. I remember the heavy silence that filled the auditorium when I learned my husband was dead. My seventeen-year-old self could never have imagined I was rehearsing a story that would someday become my own. I was memorizing the script of my own widowhood.

I thought I knew Elisabeth Elliot's story by heart. So when I found myself living my own version of it more than two decades later, I sought her as an example of how to navigate grief. I now understood the shock of sudden loss, the sorrow of losing your life partner, the responsibility of raising a child alone. I saw Elisabeth's determination to cling to life and purpose in the face of death, and I intuited that the path with grief must be a linear one from mourning to victory, that my sorrow was a wound from which I would someday heal. If she had done it, so could I, I thought.

A week after Rob's death, I discovered he had placed Elisabeth's new posthumously published book, *Suffering Is Never for Nothing*, in his Amazon cart. The book was a recommendation from his dear friend, a son of one of the martyred missionaries. Taking this as a sign, I ordered the book right away. I sensed God through Rob had given these words to me. What I discovered surprised me.

Elisabeth Elliot died in 2015, almost sixty years after her husband was speared to death on a sandbar in the jungles of Ecuador. In the years after Jim's death, Elisabeth remarried, was widowed a second time, and married again. She published more than twenty books. She enjoyed watching eight grandchildren grow. Elisabeth grew a rich, full life from the soil of the suffering she had endured.

But more than twenty years after his death, when she wrote *Suffering Is Never for Nothing*, Elisabeth still talked about Jim. A lot. His name, his story, their life together—it was all still there in the pages I held in my hands. For the rest of her life, Elisabeth could not talk about suffering, faith, purpose, or love without mentioning the man she'd loved and lost. All of her writing, from her early days of recounting his story to her final words on pain and purpose—all of her life was marked by her love for Jim. Time *changed* her grief, but it apparently had never taken it away.

What was I to make of this? For all my life I'd heard phrases like "Time heals all wounds" when people talked about losing a loved one. Here was a woman who had thrived after loss. Like the biblical Job, her life after loss had been blessed immeasurably. Nevertheless, sorrow still seemed to bear witness in everything she wrote. As I began to talk with other bereaved people, I discovered the same thing. If this was so, what could I actually expect my experience of grief to be like? I had to figure out why there was such a significant disconnect between how we talked about grief and how we actually lived it.

WHAT I THOUGHT I KNEW

When Rob died, the little I knew about grief became inadequate and unhelpful. To my surprise and disappointment, life after loss felt nothing like moving from point A to point B. Instead, each day I found myself running willy-nilly through an emotional minefield, never quite sure where grief would explode under my feet. Furthermore, my sorrow wasn't a wound. Death's bomb had detonated in the living room of my life, and everything was in shambles. A Band-Aid and time couldn't fix this. If Elisabeth Elliot was right, grief would indelibly mark me. The pathway to flourishing would be nothing like I'd expected it to be.

Few of us understand how deeply our death-averse culture has shaped how we think about the deaths of our loved ones.

Few of us understand how deeply our death-averse culture has shaped how we think about the deaths of our loved ones. The clichés we hear after loss ring hollow, and yet we're not sure we want to turn our backs on them altogether. At least they sound promising. We want to run from the reality that sorrow and suffering are endemic to this fallen world. We want to believe that we can make a way out of our grief to a better life on the other side.

However, when we allow our culture's myths and platitudes about grief and loss to seep into our thoughts and influence our actions, they actually damage us rather than console us. Honestly, grief is nothing like the talk we've heard about it. And, like it or not, God's transforming work often comes to us in suffering. We miss out on something important when we try to bypass or hurry through or explain away the hurt that shadows our path.

If we are to grieve well and live fully again, we must identify the unhealthy stories we tell and replace them with truth. We have to be honest. As we begin this journey together, we need to do some "trail maintenance" first. Let's dismantle some of these myths that create obstacles on our path and build a better, more truthful road to walk with sorrow.

MYTH #1: SOME LOSSES ARE WORSE THAN OTHERS

At first, when Rob died, I felt cheated out of the many years I believed we should have enjoyed. I had lost so much in one tragic moment; I'd never even had a chance to say goodbye. I confess that I developed a little hierarchy in my head. My children's grief was the worst: they would carry this loss for the next sixty, seventy, or eighty years of their lives. My grief came in at a close second. I isolated my suffering on a pedestal. No one could match its sorrow.

It didn't take long for these internal conversations to make me feel ashamed, and rightly so. I had to confront the exclusive claim I had laid on sorrow. My grief had bent dangerously toward selfishness. I had fallen into the world's trap of ranking grief. This wasn't a race to win the "biggest grief" award. I needed to repent of the grasping, inconsiderate attitude I had mistakenly called bereaved love.

As a corrective, I swung my emotional pendulum the other direction; I attempted to downplay the depth and breadth of my grief. Instead of comparing, I tried to convince myself that all loss was the same, that losing a good friend or an adult child was *exactly the same* as losing my husband. Even though it felt inaccurate to lump all losses together, I tried to tell myself that everybody has a cross to bear. I convinced myself there must be a silver lining I needed to find in my loss. I began to talk in "at leasts"—*at least* he wasn't sick for a long time, *at least* I knew he loved me, *at least* I had children to bear the pain beside me.

It wasn't until I talked to other grieving people that I learned how normal this back-and-forth actually is. Not only is it common to rank our own pain as worst of all, but it is also common to dismiss it altogether. Both responses derive from an innate need to understand how our grief fits into the rest of the world and how we should think about it. Come to find out, we all struggle to understand how grief can be both unique and universal—how our sorrow matters intimately to us and also in a broader context. I had looked at how the world around me talked about death and concluded that some losses must be worse than others.

Since your loved one died, have you tried to convince yourself that someone has it worse? Has a friend or family member shared a "more tragic" story with you to give you perspective? Do you feel like those around you see your loss as insignificant or your expressions of grief as overdone or unjustified? If so, you've encountered the first roadblock on your path to healthy bereavement—our culture's hierarchy of grief, the invisible ranking system we use to explain away feelings or console ourselves with platitudes.

If you've lost an elderly loved one or someone who was suffering from a terminal illness, I suspect you've encountered this hierarchy of grief as an attempt at consolation. Perhaps you've even used it to comfort yourself. We regularly use a hierarchy of grief to diminish our grief. We convince ourselves that death doesn't really need to touch us deeply, that we shouldn't be sad because Grandma "had a good, long life." We hush our grief by reasoning, "At least he has no more pain." If you've suffered a miscarriage, you might have heard hollow reassurances like

Lynn reflects on her husband's death:

My husband collapsed in the night. No goodbyes. Grief arrived swiftly and proved more complicated than what took him. Impossible to ignore, grief intruded relentlessly, interrupting with unpredictable demands. Individual needs created a fog that slowed my family. I shuttered the windows and made space to wrestle.

I laid out the challenges to trusted friends. They reassured me, "You are going to make mistakes. They are your mistakes to make." Owning my imperfection, I pleaded for God to open and close the doors guiding each step. He patiently took what I tried to let go of, over and over.

As the fog lifted, I recognized that grief was not an enemy. Although grief could not be evicted despite his rude disregard for schedules and timing, he was connected to the love that will always be part of us. In the context of love, grief refined and strengthened my family as we persevered.

"You can have another baby" or "I guess this one wasn't supposed to be." Maybe you've even said these things to yourself.

But a long life or relief from pain or a quiet, uncomplicated death does not diminish the tragedy of death. All loss deserves to be mourned. Loss of the baby you've never held is no less painful than the loss of an adult child. The death of a friend is no less heartbreaking than the death of a spouse. The death of a person who has lived out many years is just as sorrowful as the death of one we feel has had too few because *all death is a mark of the curse.* So whether it arrives early or late in life, through natural causes, an accident, or disease, death stings.

While it is true that all death is tragic, each death holds unique consequences. Different relationships elicit different grief responses and touch different dimensions of loss. I could no better understand the parent who had watched his child slowly diminished by cancer than he could understand the chaplain's visit to my campsite. A friend who lost her adult sister in a car accident couldn't grasp the radical reorienting I endured after Rob suddenly vanished from my life. My grief was indeed unique. No loss is more important than another, *and* not all grief looks the same.

No one has to live your life and grapple with the uniqueness of your grief but you. And so, as you seek to grieve freely and fully, you can allow yourself to feel that loss without explaining it away. You need not downplay your loss as "not as bad" as someone else's. You can give yourself the space to fully grieve. Even when you grieve a loss within your family, you will each grieve the unique relationship you had with that person. No one has it worse. Each person must endure their own particular loss of that person.

As you acknowledge and honor the uniqueness of your grief, your connections with others can help to ward off impulses toward self-victimization. Companions in suffering remind us not to self-isolate and nurse our wounds and not to compare our sorrows in ways that paint us as heroes or martyrs.

By directing your eyes to Jesus, you can reset the default toward a hierarchy. You walk along this difficult path with one who can fully understand the depth of your grief. Jesus, the Man of Sorrows, intimately knows abandonment, rejection, confusion, and sorrow. In the gentle companionship of his presence,

Jesus offers to wrap up your grief inside his own. He doesn't just sympathize; he empathizes. As the hymnodist writes, "Can we find a friend so faithful who will all our sorrows share?"

When you understand how beloved you are by God, how intimately known your sorrows are to him, you will discover that you don't need to be embarrassed to share your loss with those around you. In a world where it feels like you no longer belong, your grief fits perfectly in Jesus' nail-scarred hand. Because of this, you don't have to worry if you have it easier or harder than someone else who is grieving. Grief's fingerprint on your life will be your own, a sacred mark. You can release yourself from our culture's impulse to categorize our sorrows and resist the urge to dismiss your sorrow or grieve alone.

MYTH #2: THERE'S A RIGHT WAY TO GRIEVE

Because we believe that some losses deserve more attention than others, we've inadvertently bought into a system of unwritten rules that says there's a right way to grieve. Certain losses, we believe, permit certain kinds of grief. You can cry over a lost parent but not over your family's beloved pet. You can mourn your husband's death, but after a year you should move on. Keeping your loved one's belongings as they left them is just plain morose. These prescribed boundaries for grief draw the line not only between less and more painful losses. They determine when, where, and how long we should grieve. At times, they imply we shouldn't grieve at all.

After your loved one dies, you quickly learn—usually in a crash course of disaster—where and when your grief is not welcome. You find yourself apologizing for crying in public.

You worry about being a party buzzkill, so you don't mention your loss among friends. You feel compelled by those around you to complete your grief—wrap it up in a year or less, or at the very least stash it away and get back in the game. Quickly, you learn that the boundaries of grief's acceptability are very narrow.

Just a sliver of American history shows us how narrow our perspective often is when we approach how to grieve well. In my home here in New England, eighteenth-century colonial Puritans who avoided demonstrative outward displays of sorrow nonetheless threw expensive funerals that included gifts for participants and drinking that sometimes turned into drunken parades through the streets. Despite their austere theology of God's providence, Puritans "even prayed that their grief would 'never wear off,'" writes historian David Hackett Fischer. In a culture where death was commonplace and faith was bedrock, people still wrestled with how to express their losses and how long they should feel the effects.

Around the world, too, grief finds a wide variety of expressions. Many Asian cultures rely on a traditional rhythm of personal grief practices, while African communities on the continent and Black communities here in the West emphasize corporate grief. Some cultures focus on release from earth's pain, while others commit to mourning practices that would elsewhere be considered protracted. If you've felt the pressure to grieve in a particular way, be assured: it's only one of many you could choose.

The body of Christ reflects diversity of culture, tradition, and belief. It also can reflect diversity of grief expression. There is no single, definitive ritual for how to express sorrow to the glory of God. Whether or not your person's death "broke the rules" of cultural expectation, you can find assurance that seeking God's face, not others' approval, is the right way to grieve. For most of us, clearing this obstacle simply comes from hearing those words of release and permission. You are unique; your expressions of sorrow are too. As you seek physical, emotional, and spiritual health, the way you choose to express your grief can be a gift to the body of Christ.

MYTH #3: WHAT DOESN'T KILL YOU MAKES YOU STRONGER

If there is no single right way to grieve, can there be a wrong way to grieve? For the Christian, yes. Unfortunately, many of us have adopted an idea of rugged American individualism that adversity is a test of our mettle. When it comes to grief, we can mistakenly believe that how we navigate grief will show us what we're worth. Like a shot of liquor that burns as it goes down, we assert that what doesn't kill us makes us stronger. When we adopt this perspective, we're veering dangerously off course.

I understand our innate desire to forge strength from adversity. We want to believe that we can get through hard things. In a very human sense, we want assurance that our suffering isn't for nothing, that something good waits for us on the other side of it, that even the loss of someone we love has a purpose—not just in some distant future, but here and now. We turn Scripture verses about endurance into motivational sound bites meant to urge us on through our pain, often without acknowledging its full weight. In a culture where weakness and softness aren't virtues, we often feel the need to struggle forward even when the burden of grief brings us to our knees.

As Christians, we fully believe that God brings beauty from ashes, that resurrection is always his joyful gift after death. Scripture promises us that "endurance produces character, and character produces hope." We are told that "our present sufferings are not worth comparing with the glory that will be revealed in us." Science even confirms this biblical truth. Multiple research studies tell us that some lifetime adversity can result in resilience and life satisfaction. A little fire in our lives can burn away the dross and reveal gold.

> *Grief is not a strength-building exercise or an object lesson. We meet Jesus not only in triumph but in suffering. Our vulnerability in grief reveals Christ's strength abounding in us. It is not in our strength but in our weakness where we discover him mighty to save.*

However, the purpose of grief is not to function as emotional calisthenics, strengthening our heart and soul's muscles, fortifying us for whatever life throws at us. Self-reliance is not one of the fruits of the Spirit. The obstacle course of sorrow can become a very human attempt to beat back the darkness instead of seek Christ in it. Grief is not a strength-building exercise or an object lesson. We meet Jesus not only in triumph but in suffering. Our vulnerability in grief reveals Christ's strength abounding in us. It is not in our strength but in our weakness where we discover him mighty to save.

Grief may make you grow a thicker shell or get tougher. But

honestly, that's not what most of us want. We don't want our lives to be forever frozen in time, our feet stuck in the concrete of a painful past that we can never undo. Instead, we long for the freedom of a future with promise. With the Good Shepherd and grief as our companions, we can invite sorrow to mature us, to make us wiser and more tender in all the very best ways. If we are willing, our suffering will transform us into softer, gentler, more compassionate people, believers who are more accepting of weakness, more willing to sit with contradiction and mystery. This difficult path can help us develop courage and bravery, not as we prove our own strength but as we throw ourselves fully on God's.

MYTH #4: TIME HEALS ALL WOUNDS

We're highly scheduled people. We know the Monday Night Football schedule and when our favorite television drama airs each week. Our calendars rule our daily lives. We mourn that time flies when we're having fun, that the days are long but the years are short. So why wouldn't we also believe that time could have a magical effect on the sorrow we carry with us? We crave linear narratives. We want to believe that if we can just get far away enough from the event of our loss, we will find that it hurts less than it used to.

To convince ourselves of time's healing power, we often compare our grief to a wound. It certainly hurts like one, and because of sin's curse we long for pain to be fixed. We talk about being broken, about longing for healing, about pursuing recovery. But grief is not a problem in need of repair, like a broken arm or leg. It is as natural and normal as childbirth or

Grief moves not in a direct line

from point A to point B but

along a path with twists and

turns that can't be charted.

Grief comes in waves, not

cycles or predictable patterns.

breathing. Grief is not an illness or an injury. It is not inherently good or bad.

Viewing grief as an illness or injury just doesn't work. The analogy breaks down pretty quickly. Try as we might, we cannot fix sorrow. We try new relationships to fill the hole our loved one left but discover that the sadness follows us. We get discouraged that months or even years later, our hearts still feel undone and tears rise up unbidden. We expect that we should be over this—that we should be healed by now. We start to walk faster in an attempt to create distance between ourselves and grief but find that it still feels like walking on a broken leg. Why is this? Because grief is not a wound but an expression of the wounded heart.

Grief moves not in a direct line from point A to point B but along a path with twists and turns that can't be charted. It has an emotional intelligence and internal compass all its own. Grief comes in waves, not cycles or predictable patterns. And so time has little effect on the overall nature of our sorrow. Our grief ages, like a wine, maturing in flavor and adjusting in potency. But it doesn't ever go away. Time may change our grief, but it won't make it disappear.

After Rob died, everywhere I looked, I saw death and grief. However, as time passed, I found that my life began to grow around my loss. This realization terrified me. As dreadful as that night at my campsite had been, I didn't want to get too far away from it. I never wanted to forget the searing pain and hollowness I felt in my body when I received the news that Rob was dead. To leave that somehow meant to leave him behind. I discovered that as my life began to move forward with grief, I didn't want time to heal a wound.

Feeling that acute pain made me feel close to Rob. If time healed death's wound, Rob would fade further and further into my past. I couldn't bear the thought of being far away from the man I loved. I scrambled to access those piercing feelings, but I couldn't. My grief was an expression of my love. Were my love and my sorrow fading away?

One day, I opened my lockbox to grab a new book of checks. As I thumbed through the labeled envelopes, I saw the one labeled "Rob—Death." Inside, the green death certificate was folded neatly, along with the receipt for the gravestone I'd purchased. I won't tell you that all the emotions of that first night came rushing back. They didn't. But as I carefully unfolded the death certificate and read those words again—*fall . . . traumatic injuries . . . married*—I felt that familiar ache. In the middle of an ordinary day, I was again that woman on the phone talking to the medical examiner's office. I was that wife wondering what she was going to do for the rest of her life without him. My life had indeed grown full and beautiful around my loss, and *all the grief was still there.*

After our person dies, the minutes continue to tick by. Our lives continue, even when we feel—or wish—they had stopped. Over time, you will discover that you wear the weight of your grief differently. It will take up a different space in your life. Grief's newness may wear off, but its essence remains. For the rest of our lives, we will miss the one we lost. We will experience pain when we remember their absence. Time will change our pain, but we do not need to look for healing to find happiness.

We do not need to crave grief's closure to discover flourishing. We can leave the platitudes and myths behind and discover friendship in the most unexpected place. We can learn to embrace our grief.

FOR YOUR OWN REFLECTION

1. What myths have you heard or believed about grief? Do they appeal to you? If so, why?

2. Is it hard for you to acknowledge your grief as both unique and universal? Why or why not? What ways can you find to embrace this truth?

3. What expressions of grief feel most natural to you?

4. How does it make you feel to hear that time doesn't heal all wounds?

5. Where do you think Jesus might be seeking your company in your suffering?

CHAPTER 3

Meeting Grief: Getting to Know Your New Companion

She was no longer wrestling with her grief, but could sit down with it as a lasting companion and make it a sharer in her thoughts.

GEORGE ELIOT, *MIDDLEMARCH*

Six months later, it's quiet in the house. My parents have graciously offered to take my four children out for a day of adventures, and for the first time in a long time, I'm alone. Lately I've felt the weight of parenting after loss, and I want my kids to feel some of that old "normal" again. So I have bundled them up in cozy hats and gloves and kissed them at the door as they scrambled out for a morning at a local maritime museum with Grammie and Grampie.

I now stand in the front hall. The clock, a wedding gift from years ago, softly ticks in the dining room. The dishwasher hums as it works in the kitchen. And suddenly, I feel very small. Very alone. I feel Rob's absence so much it hurts deep in my body. The tears begin to fall unbidden.

I've avoided this—being away from my children—since Rob died. There's a comfort in their presence, a companionship in the sorrow that has befallen us. More than anyone else on earth, these four little people understand all that we have lost. No explanations are needed when I'm with them. I need not soften my grief to make them feel more at ease. I watch my parents' car back out of the driveway, and I want to run after them. "Take me with you!" I want to call. "Don't leave me here alone!"

If I'm honest, I know I'm not alone at all. And this is what frightens me most. Grief is here with me. In the stillness of my now empty house. In the quiet of this life that, distractions removed, aches with the gnawing of my sorrow. On every other day the noise and fullness of life with four children drowns out grief's voice. But today, in the quiet, I know I will hear her speak. I don't want to listen. I don't want to hear what grief has to say.

I set about to make good use of time, an exercise in industry and distraction. "Snap out of it, Clarissa," I tell myself. "You've wanted this for the kids." All the bereavement support resources have told me to move my body, so I do. Soon, the laundry soaks, the living room stands tidy, and my grocery list waits beside my purse by the front door. Now what?

There are activities I've learned to avoid since Rob's death, movements and rhythms that trigger my sorrow. I once took long, hot showers to wake up in the morning; now I pop in and out. Just a few months out from his death, I haven't had the heart to move Rob's soap from the dish in the shower.

However, standing in the shower with it, I feel awkwardly trapped as though we're two parties on an elevator who aren't sure whether to make eye contact. I don't even want to be alone with soap.

In less isolated locations, I feel uncomfortable too. When I empty the dishwasher after dinner—a job we used to do together—I turn on music. I suspect grief wants to speak to me in the quiet choreography of shelving cups and plates. I'm afraid that if I listen, I won't be able to function anymore, that the flood of her words will wash me away in an endless sea of tears. What could grief say that would be of any help anyway?

A NEW PARADIGM

If grief isn't a wound or an injury, if it isn't a distance event with a finish line up ahead, what is it? What is this that has arrived at your doorstep and taken up residence in every corner of your life? The sorrow you feel after losing a loved one is so powerful and so life-shaping it can be personified. Grief is your companion.

Whether or not you've recognized it as such, I know you've felt it. You've wandered into a big-box store where you thought you'd be anonymous only to meet grief face-to-face in the whiff of cologne from a passerby. You've returned to the office after the funeral to find colleagues who once rubbed elbows with you now offer extra space between your chair and theirs. They see your invisible visitor. Grief has come to work with you.

You may never have thought or heard of grief as a companion before, but I'm convinced we need this new paradigm of companionship for two reasons. First, we need words to describe how grief really operates in our lives. The longer we live with it, the more we discover that grief is persistent, all encompassing, and long lasting. It isn't static but grows and changes with us over time. Envisioning grief as a companion allows us to release the striving and resistance that character- ize so much of contemporary bereave- ment. We can turn to our grief with compassion, listen to her sorrows, and learn from her wisdom. If you're look- ing for progress, this is what it actually looks like.

> *While we are busy trying to outrun or heal or recover from our sorrows, Jesus invites us to a better way— not to avoid sadness but to befriend it.*

Second, as we acknowledge, accept, and, yes, even embrace grief, this unwel- come companion can offer us hope for the future. Like Much-Afraid in *Hinds' Feet on High Places*, when we take the hands of Sorrow and Suffering, we can walk beside them toward the life we long for after loss. New life will come in fits and starts, but to our surprise, we can move forward, not by shaking off grief but by taking her along for the journey. Befriending our grief can be the key to finding flourishing again. Isaiah 53 tells us that Jesus would be "acquainted" with grief, a word that in Hebrew can be translated "familiar friend." While we are busy trying to outrun or heal or recover from our sorrows, Jesus invites us to a better way—not to avoid sadness but to befriend it. By gently companioning our grief, we can follow in Jesus' footsteps.

If you've been wrestling with God's existence or power or love in the midst of your loss, I think you'll find relief in this new picture of your life with sorrow. The idea of grief as a companion invites you to release expectations and platitudes that reflect a narrow gospel—a 2D flannelgraph version of death and resurrection that doesn't take into account the complexities of living in a world that remains under the curse of sin. And with an experienced friend like Jesus beside you, you can step into a fuller story, one in which you can learn to trust God in new, intimate ways in the midst of your darkness, as you wait with hope for what is "not yet."

God gave us grief as a way to express what is lost. For the bereaved believer, then, the task is not to dismiss this emotion, any more than we would silence our impulses to love or anger. Instead, we can turn to grief, assured that God can offer grace through it. Knowing that God gave us the capacity for deep sorrow, we can use even this difficult gift as an opportunity to know him more.

The word *companion* literally means "with bread"—someone with whom we eat. So what if we settled in and accepted that grief isn't going anywhere? What could it teach us? How would it guide and change us? Instead of running away, let's meet this new companion and learn to think relationally about our grief. Let's sit down and do lunch together.

As you learn to welcome grief, to listen when it speaks, to acknowledge its presence in the outside world, and to accept its changing nature, I am convinced you will discover you can live as you never thought you could, even as you walk sorrow's path. You will know God's presence in new ways as he speaks to you through the emotions he has graciously given you to acknowledge and process your loss.

MAKING FRIENDS WITH GRIEF

Grief overwhelms us when she arrives and we first feel the weight of sorrow at her presence. Grief makes herself at home in our living rooms, invites herself into the kitchen, and introduces herself to our friends. Her aggressiveness perplexes us. She demands to be noticed and heard. What is a person to do with such a forward, unwelcome guest? How could our lives suddenly be consumed with loss? Life as we knew it before has vanished in a moment.

In the days that follow immediately after loss, grief demands our attention to the exclusion of other priorities. Her presence may affect our health, our stamina, and our mental fortitude. Grief may force us to question long-held beliefs. So how do we befriend this bull in the china shop? It's actually surprisingly simple.

First, companionship means that we acknowledge the holistic nature of grief's presence. Like any new addition to your home, grief affects every dimension of your life—physical, emotional, psychological, relational, spiritual, and practical. Because of this, there's no need to attempt to compartmentalize your sorrow. You can stop apologizing for crying. You can admit that you've lost your appetite. You can adjust your schedule, your household, and any other necessary parts of your life to accommodate this new friend. If you've tried to maintain your regular schedule with this intrusive new friend around, I hope hearing this brings relief.

Companionship also means that we seek relational interaction with our grief. We engage instead of ignore her. We sit down and attend to her instead of pushing her away. Because we believe that God has given us grief as a gift of emotional expression, we can meet her with the expectation that God will speak to us through her, teaching us about ourselves and gently guiding us toward becoming more like Jesus. If you've been running away, pushing away, or ignoring the weight of your sorrow, you can unclench your fists and relax your body and your mind. Inviting grief in actually is easier than holding her at bay.

Finally, the paradigm of companionship welcomes us to integrate our loss in ways that honor how our love persists beyond death. Your person may have died a week ago, a year ago, or ten years ago, but your grief doesn't need to end, because grief is an expression of love that remains after the object is gone. The companionship of grief reminds us that as our lives grow around our loss, there remain myriad ways to celebrate and honor this love, in sadness and in the joy that can grow over time. Our relationship with grief can become a healthy, normal connection point with our loved one that we carry with us into the new lives we build after our loss.

Your grief can become the place where Jesus uniquely meets and ministers to you. In your sorrow, you can find him infinitely more beautiful and gracious even as you hold the mystery of suffering and his goodness in the same hand.

All this talk of companionship raises the question, *Do I have to like this? Do I have to pretend to feel hospitable when I really wish all the sadness would go away?* Simply, no. Your relationship with grief is, no doubt, a begrudging one. You may resent your sorrow, finding it provokes anger or deep regret. That's totally normal. Remember: as much as grief is a beautiful capacity given to us by God, its expression is tied inextricably to the curse of sin.

You don't have to like your grief. All you need to do is let it in the front door of your life. Just stop ignoring the doorbell. Take that bold step and put your hand in sorrow's hand. As hard as it might be to believe right now, God will use grief to comfort, teach, encourage, and even inspire you. Sit with that thought for a bit. This isn't silver-lining talk but gospel beauty. Your grief can become the place where Jesus uniquely meets and ministers to you. In your sorrow, you can find him infinitely more beautiful and gracious even as you hold the mystery of suffering and his goodness in the same hand.

LIFE WITH GRIEF

When we encounter grief for the first time, we're much like parents welcoming a new baby. We take the cultural expectations we know and the emotions hardwired into us, and we let them lead us, much the way new parents dog-ear the pages of *What to Expect When You're Expecting*. We may have some head knowledge but little to no practical experience.

However, as parents quickly learn, you don't get to know someone through books but through engagement. This is your primary task—to get to know your grief. Especially during the acute, early days of loss (you define what "early" means to you), spending intimate time with grief is time well spent. Grief's introduction to your life may involve chaos, fumbling, frustration, anger, and moments of despair. All of this is normal.

The night the chaplains visited my campsite, I met grief in all of her shocking horror—terror, confusion, weeping, gut-wrenching pain. I was overwhelmed. My acute early grief behaved much like a newborn. She cried seemingly for hours on end. She needed lots of sleep; she quickly consumed any energy I had. Newborn grief was self-centered—not selfish but self-preserving. In the first weeks after Rob died, I tried to wrap my mind around the tragic reality of his accident, and I could think of little else. I had to be reminded even to eat and shower. In the same way that a newborn baby demands his parents' attention, my sorrow cried out to be heard, seen, and cared for.

In the Notes app on my phone, I keep a letter I wrote to myself six weeks after Rob died. It's roughly written, a series of bullet points without a salutation. I was still reeling from the shock of what had happened. I wanted to scream, to stick my fingers in my ears, curl into a ball, and disappear. I wanted to wake up from this nightmare and discover Rob alive again beside me. Most days, sorrow made me sick to my stomach. Grief's power terrified me. I knew I couldn't outrun the harrowing experience I was enduring. So, on that Sunday less than two months after Rob's death, I sat down and tried to listen for the first time to what grief had to say.

I don't remember how long it took me, but I laid it all out there. My thumbs flew as I wrote the frustration and sadness and confusion of my grief, a rush of sorrow that I could no longer dam. As I poured out my pain, I realized that for the last six weeks I'd tried to be strong. Survival mode had kicked in right away, and all my mama-bear instincts had taken over to protect and care for my children in the midst of our loss. I'd wept until I felt like I would vomit. I'd slept for hours as grief

Michael reflects on the deaths of his parents and brothers:

I lost my dad when I was twenty-five years old. In the twenty years that followed, I lost both of my brothers at thirty-eight and forty-five years old, respectively, and then my mom, leaving me in my midforties as the last person in my birth family.

Because of the grief I'd already walked through, I honestly thought I'd be better at it than I am, better at walking through the recent loss of my mom. But each loss is different from the last and hurts in new and unexpected ways.

Grief comes at unexpected moments. A song, a smell, even the sound of my own laugh can trigger it. Grief can wake me in the middle of the night, sobbing and gasping for air. It can settle in like fog over my thoughts for hours, days, weeks, and months at a time. I have lost hair because of grief, lost sleep because of grief, nearly lost friendships because of grief. I've also learned to live life more fully, chase my dreams, and overcome my fears because of grief.

Grief has made me stronger. A lot of good has come from it. But you'd better believe I'd trade it all for one more day with my dad, my brothers, and my mom.

overwhelmed my body. I'd lain awake playing solitaire on an iPad to stave off the nightmares. I'd greeted guests at the funeral and pushed down fears that I'd panic. I'd returned to my house and slept in my bed without my husband.

But I hadn't let grief really speak until that moment. It was time to release my finger from the dike, to unloose grief's tongue and let her say what she needed to say. I'd said a few of those things piecemeal to friends and family, but I'd never said it all like this. That day as I put words to the sorrow that was consuming me, grief found her voice.

In the days that followed, I discovered that grief voiced my longings, my frustrations, my pain, and my love. Much to my surprise, grief spoke her mind without embarrassment. As I turned my attention to my sorrow, I found that I no longer needed to push away the feelings that came naturally throughout my day. The commuter train whistled as I sat in my car in the school drop-off line, and I heard grief lament, "Rob was supposed to drop the kids off at school in the morning before he caught the train." As I sat alone in my Sunday school class at church, an empty seat beside me, grief whispered, "Remember how he used to slip his arm around your shoulders as you sat side by side?" When a friend complained about her husband's annoying bathroom habits, grief grumbled frustratedly, "At least he's alive." Allowing grief to speak was easier than shushing it all the time.

As you begin to open to grief as your companion, I invite you to take the time and space to acknowledge the depth and breadth of your loss. Like you would when meeting a new friend, sit with your sorrow long enough to develop intimacy. How does your grief feel in crowds and when alone? What old fears and insecurities does your sorrow conjure up? When grief shares her anger or frustration, can you listen respectfully and with an open mind?

AS TIME PASSES

When my friend Carol's daughter became engaged twelve years after her father died, Carol couldn't have been happier.

She wasn't a giddy woman, but she often felt like she'd drunk champagne. Since her husband Phil's death over a decade ago, Carol had prayed that her children would thrive after their sudden, devastating loss. Her daughter's upcoming marriage to a wonderful young man felt like an answer to that prayer.

The days before the wedding were a flurry of joyful activity, and Carol happily assisted wherever she was able. The wedding would be held at a beautiful lakeside retreat center where the family had vacationed for years. The location held special memories for the whole family. Standing at the water's edge, you could almost hear the years' laughter echo across the lake. The family had grieved together there too. After Phil's death, they'd sprinkled his ashes along the shoreline. When I talked to Carol a few days before the wedding, she was ebullient. She anticipated a day filled with joy and celebration; her family was expanding in the best of ways.

I didn't hear from Carol for a few weeks after the wedding weekend, but I thought nothing of it. Big celebrations are exhausting. I was sure she needed some downtime. When we talked again, I was surprised. Carol hadn't been relaxing; she'd been grieving. "The day was filled with so many happy memories of Phil," Carol told me as she teared up. Her daughter had remembered her father in beautiful, poignant ways on her special day. But through all the joy of the ceremony and reception, there wove a sorrow that surprised Carol with its power. Thirteen years later, she felt Phil's absence palpably, deeply, painfully. As her daughter walked down the aisle to violins, grief sang her own quiet song. As friends and family laughed and danced late into the night, grief reclined at a table in the

Grief not only expresses

our despair and sorrow.

She offers comfort, wisdom,

and a powerful connection

to the love that continues

after death.

reception hall. Even many years later, grief was still Carol's companion.

As we accustom ourselves to grief as a companion, we watch her change. She still spouts frustration and anger from time to time, but we're surprised to find her often thoughtful, measured, wise, and loving. Grief may no longer make outbursts at family dinners or work meetings, but she's still there. We know this because every time an unsuspecting friend or neighbor makes a comment, we still wince. At birthday celebrations and graduations, we still long for the empty chair to be filled once again. Grief remains quiet but present always.

As the years pass, the initial moment of our acutest pain fades into the rearview mirror. Your family may be far away from that night long ago when the chaplain arrived at your door, when the doctor told you there was nothing more he could do, when you said your last goodbyes. While the loss is still as real and significant as ever, the pain feels different. Something has shifted. Grief has matured.

After years of grief's companionship, you might be tempted to think you've actually completed the famous five stages of grief. Grief *is* linear, after all! You're done. And then your daughter walks down the aisle or your son becomes a father or your best friend loses his wife, and the pain that still lies deep inside rises like a tsunami, unexpectedly powerful and unable to be stopped. Once again, you feel at the mercy of grief's force.

Especially in these seasons, we can find reassurance in acknowledging grief as a companion. This emotion given to us by God continues to help us make sense of love when it is lost.

Years later, it still speaks. In the same way that we don't need to "get over" fear to live happily, we can learn to live and adapt to our lives with grief. No relationship remains static, and we can expect this of our relationship with grief as well. When we get over the need to get over our sorrow, we are able to welcome it into our lives as a signifier of something larger. Particularly as grief matures, we can find wisdom as we listen to her.

Grief not only expresses our despair and sorrow. She also offers comfort, wisdom, and a powerful connection to the love that continues after death. When we turn to grief and receive her wisdom, we invite God to speak into the most painful places of our lives. When we invite grief to participate in our lives, we discover that rather than dragging us down, grief has inherent strengths—wisdom that has been gained through the fire. Through suffering we meet Jesus intimately. In a mysterious way, even in the pain there can be a gift. This companionship that we once feared would crush us can deepen our love, strengthen our belief, and embed hope deep within us.

As grief matures, it becomes familiar, more bearable. It adapts with us. Because grief and love are so closely connected, we learn to do both simultaneously. We learn to acknowledge and welcome other companions—joy, contentment, hope, and love. Grief's presence reminds us every day of all that is wrong with the world. By doing so, grief points us forward. We do not sorrow as those who have no hope. One day, grief will not simply depart; it will be transformed. Mourning will turn to dancing. Garments of praise will replace our sackcloth and ashes.

OTHER COMPANIONS ON THE PATH

After our loved ones die, grief moves into our homes, but it's not the only companion who has made a home with us. We are made of many parts. And while grief touches and colors every place of our lives, if we are to survive and thrive again, we must acknowledge, welcome, and nurture these other parts as well. Courage. Thoughtfulness. Adventure. Persistence. Love.

The mystery of grief's companionship is that her presence highlights so many other parts of our lives to which we once paid little attention. Hannah Hurnard describes Much-Afraid's realization like this:

> It seemed as though her senses had been quickened in some extraordinary way, enabling her to enjoy every little detail of her life; so that although her companions actually were Sorrow and Suffering, she often felt an almost inexplicable joy and pleasure at the same time.

No doubt, achievements are harder won after loss. Life is tinged with sadness. All of our different parts will forever be informed by grief. It has shaped us powerfully. Grief has important things to say around our tables, important truths about love and life and perspective to speak into our lives. But grief is not the only voice that speaks into our lives post-loss. In surprising inbreakings, joy does too. Joy will travel with us also—sometimes holding hands awkwardly with grief, other times walking far ahead of the crowd, leading the way. Joy, like grief, will make herself indispensable.

Joy's presence after loss can only be described as beautifully disruptive. Its arrival can be just as jarring and puzzling. We're not expecting it at all. And then laughter bubbles up after the funeral. Our new grandbaby smiles for the first time, and we can't help but smile back. Life draws us forward, and we discover we are walking hand in hand with grief *and* joy. The one informs and deepens the other.

As you take the hand of grief, I invite you to welcome all these companions to walk with you.

Consider the truth that grief may offer you a unique perspective and gateway to a rich life that you never could have imagined. All these parts of you are essential to abundant life in the face of loss.

The path with grief is not an easy one. Her presence will break, shape, and refine you as you never could have imagined. But I'm convinced that grief is not a companion we need to fear. Grief is not only how we make sense of our loved ones' deaths; it is the vehicle by which we express our longing for all things to be made new. By befriending grief, we reject toxic positivity, acknowledge the full weight of sin's curse, and direct our eyes to Jesus. To our surprise, grief can guide us gently through darkness to gospel hope.

FOR YOUR OWN REFLECTION

1. If you were to imagine grief as a person, how would you describe him or her?

2. How do you feel about grief's companionship with you today?

3. What is one way you could make more space for grief in your life?

4. Think over the last twenty-four hours. What other companions joined you in your day?

5. Where do you think Jesus wants to meet you as you walk hand in hand with grief?

PART 2

TOOLS

FOR

SURVIVAL

CHAPTER 4

Aching Bones and Sleepless Nights: Physical Dimensions of Loss

Love has gone and left me and the days are all alike;
Eat I must, and sleep I will,—and would that night were here!
But ah!—to lie awake and hear the slow hours strike!
Would that it were day again!—with twilight near!

EDNA ST. VINCENT MILLAY, "ASHES OF LIFE"

After I arrived home, back across the country, from Rob's funeral and memorial services, a church friend began coordinating meals for our family. Three nights a week, folks from our congregation arrived bearing delicious dinners for the kids and me. I'll never forget how thoughtfully chosen those meals were. My children loved the "tacos in a bag"—totable Mexican dinners in single-serving bags of Doritos. They devoured the cartons of fruit from the Sunday school teacher's garden and the ice cream treats from dear friends on a hot summer night. My four growing children gobbled down every meal, and I was grateful. I'd lost all energy for cooking, and many times I could barely eat a bite. Rob's death had dealt a blow to my digestive system.

From the first days after his death, I struggled to eat regularly. Foods I once couldn't put down now lacked appeal. Many days I stood looking into the refrigerator and coached myself, "You have to eat *something*." I saw my life reflected in the stacks of Tupperware containers—a life once delightfully satisfying, now just scraps. Grief whispered, "*You're* what's left over now." I had known for many years that the brain and gut were connected, but I experienced it in new measure with grief sitting beside me at the dinner table.

Grief reveals to us, sometimes for the first time, that our emotions and bodies are intimately connected. We experience loss in our stomachs, our muscles, and our brains. It's not unusual to be surprised by how much grief affects your body after the death of your loved one. At first, you may feel like you're barely hanging on to your health and sanity. Sometimes you can feel so worn down that you fear you might die too.

It's common for people to experience physical problems after losing a loved one. Often we don't talk about this because the intimacy of talking about our bodies embarrasses us or we worry that loss will beget other loss. We may have heard of people "dying of a broken heart," and we fear the same could happen to us. However, as we begin this walk with grief as our companion, we need to understand how grief's presence affects us and how we can adapt. We can learn to sit with the pain in our bodies, offer ourselves the care we need in this critical time, and meet Jesus in new ways through our suffering.

ALL THE WAYS YOU LEFT ME

When your loved one dies, you lose their presence in every moment in which you would have interacted. Did you meet your son for breakfast every Friday morning before work? Your stomach misses him when you eat alone in the café. Did your mother rub your back when you were sick? Your shoulders and muscles remember her when you take ill and she's not there. Did you slip beneath the sheets each night beside your spouse? Your whole body longs for him or her—his caress, her warmth, his strength.

In early, acute grief, we discover the multitude of ways death has physically separated us from our person. Gone is the maker of meals, the companion at dinner, the diet accountability partner. One side of the bed grows cold at night where your sexual partner used to lie. Even before you've fully comprehended the sweeping loss of your person, your body knows he or she is gone.

Grief invades every physical space. It's common after the death of a loved one to experience changes in appetite, sleep, energy, and mental aptitude.

Grief invades every physical space. It's common after the death of a loved one to experience changes in appetite, sleep, energy, and mental aptitude. You may discover that your hearty appetite has shrunk away, leaving you to push food around your plate at mealtimes, or you may turn to food for comfort. Digestive troubles like nausea, irritable bowel syndrome, or constipation reflect the body's stress as it processes your loss. Every cell of your body is calling out for care.

Bereaved people often complain of muscle aches and tension, even phantom, ambiguous pain. You may experience immune vulnerabilities or higher blood pressure than normal because of stress or chemical changes and low sex drive as you adjust to your loved one's absence. If your person attended doctor visits with you to offer support or provided a sounding board for you to process health symptoms, these bodily changes can feel even more scary and overwhelming.

LEAN IN, LET GO, LET GOD

When I began training for the Chicago Marathon in the spring of 2010, I discovered to my surprise that the training schedule didn't involve running every day. On the contrary, running would comprise three to four days a week, while strength training filled the alternate days. This rhythm puzzled me. Wouldn't I naturally become stronger if I ran every day? Wasn't long-distance endurance the goal? I didn't realize that my success on race day depended on holistic preparation for the challenge. If I wanted to cross the finish line, every part of me would need to be ready. And ready didn't simply mean bulging muscles and a sweaty sheen. Most surprising of all, one day each week I wasn't supposed to do anything at all. Rest was essential.

Shouldering forward through grief—trying to act as though life hasn't changed—isn't healthy. As you welcome grief as your companion, you'll want to avoid unhealthy behaviors and over-extending yourself. But much research also shows that facing the hard parts of our loss builds endurance. Your body needs both rest and motivation to push through toward new life. Learning to balance these two needs on the trail with grief is key to resilience. Both types of care can be therapeutic. Your walk with grief will be a delicate dance of leaning into the hard parts of your new life and letting go for rest, repair, and renewal.

There is no magic formula to help you know when you're pushing through grief too hard and when to pull back. Honest self-assessment will tell you much of what you need. As your body adjusts to the loss of your person, you'll quickly discover your physical limits. An afternoon run around the neighborhood that used to exhilarate now exhausts. A rich pasta dinner that used to make you salivate now sends you to the bathroom with sharp stomach pains. Your body always sends you signals, and you should learn to listen to them carefully.

As you encounter these physical changes, you may find that some people don't understand your needs. They're insulted that you refuse dinner out. They insist you take seconds at a meal. They don't understand your exhaustion or become frustrated at your mental confusion. As if the task of processing grief wasn't hard enough, you've got to manage these relationships, too. You'll also discover the mercy of those who can honor your physical needs. As you're able, share your limitations with these people and lean on them for support. Create healthy boundaries with people who aren't able to offer you the space you need to let your body adjust to what you're enduring. Above all, consult your doctor if you have specific concerns about your health.

If we could fix ourselves, you'd need no further advice. But, of course, that's not the case. You can do all the "right" things for your body and still struggle. Grief's power can still wreak havoc, however hard you try. Thanks be to God we're not left alone in broken bodies with broken hearts. Jesus enters into our pain and offers rest and repair that nourish us and fortify us for the hard physical work of caring for our sorrowing bodies. As you care for your physical needs, Jesus attends to you too.

We're often told in grief to focus on the basics: eat, sleep, and exercise. Even as I write those three words, I think of how daunting they seemed in the first weeks and months after Rob died. So let's adjust them, shall we? In the early days of grief, *nourish*, *rest*, and *move*. Say those words out loud right now and take a deep breath and then slowly exhale. *Nourish. Rest. Move.* Sound easier and more manageable? I hope so. Let's discuss more.

NOURISH

After Rob's death, an acquaintance saw me in a new outfit and exclaimed, "Well, *you're* looking great!" I don't think she realized I'd dropped weight not from effort but from stress. In grief, nothing tasted the same anymore. Familiar foods reminded me of Rob, and mealtime was painful with an empty chair at the table. My new life called for a new relationship to food; I would need to change my expectations. That's when "nourish" became my touchpoint. If the road ahead would be long and arduous, it was time to gently nourish my hurting body.

Research tells us that grief's accompanying stress can depress the immune system and agitate the digestive system. With all of that strain, nourishment becomes vital. If you're struggling with appetite since your loved one died, that's okay. You can adjust your old habits to make space for grief.

Lean In

Gently care for your body in acute grief by focusing on nourishing it with foods that support healthy digestion, good mental health, and a strong immune system. Mom's old adage of eating your fruits and veggies works well here. Many grieving people appreciate meals delivered after their loved one's death. If that's you, ask for fresh foods when you're invited to make food preferences or requests known. Avoid sweets and complex carbohydrates that produce a caloric boost but leave you feeling down afterward. Grief is hard enough without the roller-coaster ride of a sugar rush.

Let Go

If the sight of food turns your stomach, take a multivitamin or try a protein shake for a little extra nutrition. Release your expectations about the food pyramid or finishing your plate. Eat what you can when you can. It's also okay to turn down offers of food. Meals often trigger difficult memories, especially in the early days of loss. If you're not ready for that, invite friends to bring restaurant gift cards or frozen dinners instead. When you're ready, you'll have their tangible support waiting to fill your belly with love.

Let God

As you take small bites of a dinner that has lost its flavor, invite Jesus to your table. Ask him to break the bread and wine of new life before you. Ask him to nourish you with his presence, to give you eyes to see his companionship with you there. If your table includes an empty chair now, envision Jesus filling that

Melissa reflects on losing her friend to cancer:

What does sorrow feel like in my body? At first, the plane hits turbulence, and I can't fight the panic anymore. I'm too deep in grief now. I've stopped remembering the feeling of good news on the other side of unexpected phone calls. I'm numb around any thought of happiness in the days to come.

Or I'm standing in a downpour at night, the rain blinding my eyes. I have to take off my glasses because they're making my vision even worse. It's hard to breathe when the wind blows, and it's been dark for a while. But we're not close to morning. I could go inside and try to dry off, to pretend the deluge isn't happening, to warm myself until I'm out of logs for the fireplace. But I know they're eventually going to burn down, and I'll have to come back outside to get more. I'll have to face this reality again.

I just want to talk to her again.

seat. If mealtime is especially quiet now, make conversation aloud with him as you eat. Savor Jesus' promise: "If anyone hears my voice and opens the door, I will come in to him and eat with him, and he with me."

REST

Since your person died, you may feel as though the world has ground to a halt. Time seems to have stopped or at least moves in slow motion. The days blur together. When you try to re-enter the flow of the life you lived before, at work or even just at Walmart, you're quickly overwhelmed. Grief requires a slower pace. You can't handle the outside world. You're just *so tired*.

Changes in energy mark grief's arrival and alert you that your body needs care. Dr. George Bonanno of the Loss, Trauma, and Emotion Lab at Columbia University writes, "Sadness dampens our biological systems so that we can pull back. Sadness slows us down and, by doing so, seems to slow the world down." What a marvel that God even uses this biological function to help us care for ourselves in suffering!

Sadness, then, isn't a bad thing. In fact, Bonanno says, sadness can function in ways that are essential to our physical adaptation after loss. Exhaustion is a natural response to help us cope. Our digestion slows, our heart rate slows, we tire more easily. As our brains work hard, our bodies long for rest. After you lose your loved one, you may discover that you need more than your regular eight hours of sleep.

Many bereaved people experience sluggishness, sometimes describing it as a fog. You may feel restless or become weary even without expending much effort. Maybe you can't remember where you've left your keys or whether you turned off the oven when you left the house. I remember driving my children to school one morning and feeling lost at a familiar intersection. My brain was so occupied with processing loss that even our regular route looked new and different. When I tried to think hard whether to go left or right, I felt worn out.

Lean In
Whether you're more tired than usual or struggling to settle in, try to maintain a sleep/wake routine. Lie down in bed on time even if you don't fall asleep. Set an alarm in the morning. Practice visualization and relaxation as ways of calming before

bed. Meditation, centering prayer, and breath prayer can offer your body physiological prompts toward relaxation, alerting your body to its need for rest. Feel free to get creative.

Let Go

Barring medicative intervention, you can't force your body to sleep, even when it's dog tired. That's why I encourage you to prioritize *rest* over *sleep*. Rest is an essential biological function. By releasing the pressure to get a full eight hours and focusing on rest, you're positioning your body in the right direction.

While excessive sleepiness and sleeplessness are both common in early grief, you may be surprised that after a day of crying hard, drowsiness doesn't seem to set in. Your mind may be in a fog or going ninety miles an hour, but sleep becomes a commodity almost impossible to find. Nightmares may make for restless, disturbing sleep. Sometimes it's hard to sleep even with a light on.

If nightmares plague you, determine a coping mechanism to help you through rough nights. Ask a friend to be your go-to for a late-night call or text. Turn on a light and rest or listen to music. Remember that the goal here is getting through. The goal is rest. It doesn't need to be pretty. If sleeping on the same sheets you slept on with your person helps you get some shut-eye, go ahead and do it. Sleep in her recliner if it allows you to close your eyes more easily. If you need to buy a new comforter or pillows, suggest it to the person who asks, "How can I help?" Save the old ones in the closet (you may want them later), and settle beneath sheets that don't hold hard reminders. Your needs may (and probably will) change as grief lives with you longer, but in these early days, it's okay for things to feel makeshift.

Perhaps getting to sleep or staying asleep isn't your struggle. Maybe the opposite is true for you. If you're feeling more tired than normal, listen to your body and sleep. Sleep restores us, enhances our immune functioning, regulates our hormones, and performs a host of other positive functions. If your body is crying out for rest, try as best as you can to give it what it needs. Disruptions in sleep patterns can be a normal part of grief, but be sure to talk with your doctor if you have concerns.

Let God

As you see the day draw to an end, invite Jesus to rest with you. Ask him to hold you with gentle strength as you close your eyes. If slowing down feels hard for you, use pictures from Scripture to help envision God's care for you. Envision yourself as a satisfied baby resting in his mother's arms (Psalm 131:2) or like a chick huddled warm and safe beneath its mother's wings (Deuteronomy 32:11). If you find it hard to turn off the light, leave a night-light on as a reminder that the one who watches over you never slumbers (Psalm 121:3-4). You can close your eyes in trust because God cares for you even in your sleep.

MOVE

A few days after Rob died, my friend encouraged me to take a walk around her neighborhood. The kids and I had holed ourselves up in their home that terrible night, and we hadn't really been outside since. The five of us put on our shoes and stepped out for a trip around the block.

I remember walking up the hill to her mailbox and needing to stop halfway to rest. The sun shone warm on my face, but my feet felt like lead. Making it to the mailbox would be a feat of mammoth proportions. My lungs shrank tight and small in my chest. I felt like I'd been trampled by a herd of bison. Grief ached in every part of my body, but something in that short walk awakened my body again. I took deep breaths of fresh air and felt the warm expanse of the sky above me. When everything felt like it was closing in, nature offered me space. I made a commitment to take a daily walk after that. In this life that felt frozen in disaster, I discovered movement helped.

We know all the benefits of regular exercise—emotional regulation, hormonal balance, cardiovascular health, and stress relief. Movement in grief holds twin purposes. First, it addresses these very physical needs. To endure this difficult path, you need to be healthy. But movement holds another purpose that I have found just as vital. Movement can make your life feel less destroyed.

I don't know if it was the endorphins firing or the metaphor of movement, but my daily walks became a joyful commitment to my overall health in grief. When I looked around at my life, I felt stuck in circumstances I never wanted, but when I walked, I felt released. I couldn't walk away from grief. Many days she walked beside me as I cried and cried. But in a world where so little felt like it was within my control anymore, I discovered that I could still put one foot in front of the other. Not fast, but deliberate. Not far, but purposeful. When I walked, I felt free again.

As I moved outside, I became more attentive to the world around me. I had to move slowly because I tired quickly, and

I found myself stopping to watch squirrels chase each other up trees. I stood in awe of the bald eagles that circled over the neighborhood lake. Contrary to every impulse I felt, the world still throbbed with vibrant life. Not *everything* was dead. Movement in nature offered me connection to a story broader than my own. It drew me out of the tight confines of my sorrow and opened my eyes afresh to a life that persistently kept going, to a cycle of death and resurrection that was written all across creation, from the dry leaves beneath my feet to the fresh green tips of new growth on the cedars along the road.

Lean In

If movement in grief feels challenging to you, start small and soft. Stretch in the morning when you wake and invite your body to move at a slow pace. Stretching relieves tension, elongates muscles, and increases blood flow to your body. If you can, spend your movement time outside. Not only will the sunlight help promote healthy circadian rhythms and subtly assist your sleep/wake routine, but you can also practice deep breathing in the fresh air—another gentle form of movement. Weed the garden and walk to get the mail, not to get the job done but as an act of loving care for your hurting body. Start with five minutes, then move up to ten or twenty or thirty minutes as you're able. If movement offers you a comforting connection with the memory of your loved one, do something you enjoyed doing together.

Let Go

Because you're moving with grief beside you, you may find memories or emotions stimulated through physical activity. This is natural and can offer healthy release. Take the time to face those emotions and offer them space as you move. If moving makes your heart sad, slow your body down, return to gentle stretching, and get extra rest if you need it.

Let God

As you take a short walk to get your mail or around the block, invite Jesus to join you as you move with grief. Ask him to reveal his beauty in the world around you, to enliven your whole body for the hard journey of living without the one you love. The Bible tells us that in God "we live and *move* and have our being." Every movement of your muscles is a gift of the Spirit. Offer a simple "thank you" as you feel your body stretch and muscles flex. God is empowering you to walk with grief.

WHEN LIFE GETS HARDER

Try as we might, nourish, rest, and move may not be enough. Grief can be a grueling companion, and the path of sorrow is an arduous one. Health and mental health changes are common after the loss of a loved one, and it's wise to acknowledge when you need more help than you can provide for yourself.

When I became a solo parent, new health concerns cropped up. I worried about my heart health, about developing cancer. I feared twinges and pains. Anxiety that I had managed naturally for years threatened me with new worries that I struggled to face on my own. I reached out to a licensed mental health counselor who specialized in grief support, but I was too frightened to go to the doctor to discuss my physical concerns. When I'd faced medical issues in the past, Rob had always come with me.

My doctor was on maternity leave, so when I finally mustered the courage to head in for a visit, I was nervous. I'd never met the provider I'd be seeing. Although she could learn my story from my records, I didn't know how she'd respond once we were together in the room. I dreaded the visit and almost canceled a couple of times because of cold feet.

When the doctor came in, her eyes met mine and filled with tears. "I can hardly look you in the eyes," she told me. "I can't imagine what you have been through." Suddenly, I knew I was in a safe space. She wouldn't provide me with just good medical care; she would care for my soul as well. I could hear the tenderness in her voice. I could see it in her tear-filled eyes.

One of the ways you can love yourself and keep loving your person is by taking care of yourself— scheduling the doctor appointment, showing up for the test, sitting on the table in that chilly exam room when you'd rather run away.

For the next thirty minutes we talked. She evaluated my symptoms, normalized my concerns, and commended my bravery in simply showing up. "After people lose their loved ones, they often avoid coming to the doctor," she told me. "I'm really glad you came in." I could honestly say I was glad too.

Going to the doctor after your person dies can be incredibly hard, whether it's having to relive the medical sights and smells and sounds or whether you're just afraid of more bad news. Being vulnerable in that little exam room can feel overwhelming. But one of the ways you can love yourself and keep loving your person is by taking care of yourself—scheduling the appointment, showing up for the test, sitting on the table in that chilly exam room when you'd rather run away. Rather than avoiding the doctor, you can seek out one who will carry your story with gentleness, who will honor your heart's pain even as she works to heal your body's. It might take a couple of tries to find the right fit, but those people are out there.

YOUR BODY REMEMBERS

When we lose our person, we lose them in a multitude of ways, but perhaps the most awkward to discuss is the intimate physical dimension of loss. When the widow says, "I miss his arms around me," we grow uncomfortable. When the widower laments his loss of bedroom intimacy, we cringe just a little. We think that "good Christians" shouldn't talk about or feel that stuff.

But if you've lost your husband or your wife, you have lost his or her body. A mother misses the weight of her child in her arms. A friend misses an embrace. And when a man loses his wife, he loses all of her—from the mundane to the sacred and intimate. When a wife loses her husband, she loses him at the kitchen table and in their marriage bed. We are bodies who love and worship and grieve.

My marriage to Rob was incarnate. When he died, I lost not just his personality or his intellect, his companionship or his wit, but flesh and bone—heat and pulse and smell and touch. I lost his hands around my waist as I stood at the sink washing dishes. His warm body against mine under the blankets at night. His hair and shoulders and sweat and strength and the million physical intimacies that those who call each other

beloved share in the sacred union of their one-flesh life. To lose
Rob has been to be physically alone in the deepest, most piercing way I know. For almost twenty years I knew my body in
relation to his.

When I think of the many ways I will lose Rob to memory,
I am afraid I will forget the feeling of his body. I never want
to forget the way it felt to have his body close to mine. Three
years later, I look at pictures of him and work hard to conjure
up those physical memories. I look at his eyes and the smile
lines that round them. I remember how it felt to be seen by
him. I look at his shoulders, and I think of how it felt to lean
against them. I look at his hands, and I remember all they held.
His beloved ax bought for the joy of hardy labor. Our newborn
babies, fresh from the womb. My hands, chilly on a winter day.
I want reassurance that Rob's presence is seared forever in my
body's memory. I'm afraid the physical knowing will slip away.

As I connect with bereaved spouses, over and over I hear this
as one of their most significant physical concerns. *I'm afraid I
will forget how his or her body felt.* If this is you, you may find
comfort in knowing that science shows us clearly that long after
someone is gone or an event has passed, our bodies can recall—
can still feel—the details. Sometimes this remembering is painful; other times it is a gift.

My body's capacity for memory surprised me after I took off
my wedding rings for good. When I first decided to take off my
bands, the nakedness almost felt wrong. I thought it would go
away eventually. However, even three years after going ringless,
I still feel a funny sensation on my left ring finger where my
bands sat for almost two decades. I often wear a different ring

to meet that sensory need. My body still knows something is missing. Sometimes I rub lotion on my hands because the feeling is so visceral. My hands remember when I was married. My body knows I am a widow now.

If your relationship with your spouse or other loved one was abusive or painful, this remembering can hurt deeply. Unbidden, hard memories may bring you back to physical touch that violated or injured you. Grief has a painful way of conjuring up our old ghosts, and as you navigate all the other physical dimensions of your loss, you'll have to face this, too. If this kind of hurt is part of your story, I encourage you to find a trusted grief counselor who can walk with you through processing this complex part of your loss. You don't need to face this hard remembering alone.

KNOWN AT THE TABLE

On a road to Emmaus, two friends met a man who embodied loss. His scarred hands spoke silent words of suffering. The wound in his side, hidden beneath his cloak, recalled deep pain and sadness. Every cell in this man's body bore the imprint of the pain he had endured.

As they walked together, the two friends introduced this man to their unseen companion—grief. Their teacher, Jesus, had died and left them confused, sorrowing, frustrated. "We had our hopes up that he was the One," they lamented, "the One about to deliver Israel." You can hear their disappointment, the abandonment that echoes in their words.

As the western sky glowed pink and purple and dusk began to fall, the two friends invited this fellow traveler inside for a

As we care for our bodies in grief, we find that we can better shoulder the burden of our sorrow. We nourish, rest, and move. And each of these simple choices to care for our physical bodies ripples out in ways that help all of our selves to adjust to new life after loss.

bite to eat. He protested politely. They insisted, "Stay and have supper with us. It's nearly evening; the day is done." Finally, he accepted.

That night, as the bread was broken and the wine poured, the two friends sat astounded and undone. They recognized the hands that broke the bread. They remembered their warmth, their gentleness, their healing strength. And the eyes that caught their gaze across the table—they recognized those, too. Who could forget them?

Grief is a demanding companion at times, and the first place we confront this is in our bodies. As we learn to survive the physical ravages of grief's arrival in our lives, we move from "barely hanging on" to learning new coping skills, much like a new mother learns to nurse her baby with her lunch plate propped on the baby's back. As we care for our bodies in grief, we find that we can better shoulder the burden of our sorrow. We nourish, rest, and move. And each of these simple choices to care for our physical bodies ripples out in ways that help all of our selves to adjust to new life after loss.

But our care for our physical bodies is not just a gardener maintaining his flower beds. As we meet grief in our bodies, Jesus invites us to meet him, too. Like the two friends on the way to Emmaus, you may struggle to find Jesus as you walk with grief. The sorrow of your loss may cry out so loudly you hardly recognize his voice as you walk along the path.

But whether or not you can see him in this time of pain, Jesus walks beside you and your grief, and he longs to meet you in the most physical places of your loss—even at the dinner table. Jesus' presence on our path of sorrow isn't just a cerebral or emotional comfort. It is a physical one too. Jesus accompanies you in the everyday challenges you face in this season of sorrow. His scarred hands remind you that he knows the physical burdens of suffering. His companionship promises you strength as you face the challenges of grief and rebuild your life after loss.

FOR YOUR OWN REFLECTION

1. Sit quietly in a chair and close your eyes. Do a slow body scan, starting from your toes and moving all the way to the top of your head. Notice how your body feels in each area. Where do you feel grief's presence?

2. Have you felt pressure to plow through your grief and keep going? What kind of a toll is it taking on your body? What parts of your everyday life need to change to offer you space to care for your body?

3. How has your eating changed since your person died?

4. We need both rest and movement in acute grief. How can you add these two rhythms to your daily schedule?

5. Have you taken advantage of community grief support like support groups or counseling? If not, what holds you back? How might these resources offer you new tools in your grief support toolbox?

CHAPTER 5

Bushwhacking through the Forest: Navigating the Practical Dimensions of Loss

When someone you love dies, and you're not expecting it, you don't lose her all at once; you lose her in pieces over a long time—the way the mail stops coming, and her scent fades from the pillows and even from the clothes in her closet and drawers. Gradually, you accumulate the parts of her that are gone. Just when the day comes—when there's a particular missing part that overwhelms you with the feeling that she's gone, forever—there comes another day, and another specifically missing part.

JOHN IRVING, A PRAYER FOR OWEN MEANY

One of my all-time favorite *I Love Lucy* scenes finds Lucy and Ethel wrapping candies on the assembly line in a chocolate factory. When the conveyor belt starts, the two women smile at their early success. "This is easy!" Lucy remarks. "Yea, we can handle this okay," Ethel adds. But they can't revel in their success too long because the belt speeds up.

As chocolates stream out, the women grow nervous. "I think we're fighting a losing game," Lucy says as she begins popping chocolates in her mouth. She's right. Soon the women are inundated. They frantically scoop chocolates into their hats and stuff them down their dresses and into their mouths to try to hide the evidence. The situation has become dreadfully out of control. They can't cope with the pace.

After death arrives, our lives may come to a standstill, but around us the world seems to pick up speed. We may want to stay in bed all day, but bills wait to be paid and meals to be made. There's a person's life to pack up and put away; there are finances and holidays and tasks to be addressed. Responsibilities stream down life's conveyor belt one after another. In early grief, we scramble to keep up.

Life after loss involves many radical shifts, especially for those who have lost someone within their immediate household, such as a child or spouse. The death of our loved one may thrust us into new roles for which we were not prepared. We become bookkeeper and accountant, household manager or impromptu holiday host.

Whether we scramble to develop new skills on the fly or realize we must delegate responsibilities, flourishing will require us to find ways to articulate our grief and lean on those who can support and walk with us on this hard path. You'll encounter myriad demands as you close down the life of your person and move forward, but you can develop a plan. You can learn to take grief with you and navigate with her in every sphere of your life.

WHY IS THIS SO HARD?

In the last chapter, we talked about how grief affects our bodies, but we didn't discuss perhaps the most prominent place our loss affects us—our brains. Many recently bereaved people

I talk to complain that grief has hijacked their brains, and I can think of few better analogies for what happens. In the hours and days following the death of our loved ones, grief slides into our cerebral driver's seat and steps on the gas. Where we thought we were going matters little to grief. She's got her own plan.

"Grief brain" is a common phenomenon in early bereavement, but we talk little about the confusion and frustration it causes. New, acute grief demands your brain's circuits work at high capacity, and this increase in workload can affect both short-term and long-term memory. You might find yourself forgetting names or appointments. You may become distracted or confused while driving. You may struggle with transitions that used to feel normal, like leaving the house or grocery store. Many people complain that the fog of early grief clouds certain memories about the events surrounding their loss.

If you had experienced these things pre-loss, you might have worried you were going senile. I know that many times I worried, *What has happened to me? Am I going insane?* As your brain works hard to process your loss and the adjustments that must come with it, everything can feel out of whack. Be encouraged, though. In time the fog will most likely fade as you adjust to life without your person. In the meantime, taking basic steps to organize your life will offer light as you navigate this new terrain. Even in these hard days and months, you can address the practical dimensions of your loss.

DOES ANYBODY EVEN KNOW I'M GRIEVING?

For the first three months after Rob died, anytime I went out in public, I chose to wear black and avoid using makeup. I needed a way to embody my sorrow. Each morning for three months I put on those black clothes. When my son mistakenly used bleach in a load of laundry instead of detergent, I wore the mottled black tank top anyway. Short of writing "I feel dead inside" across my forehead, how else could I communicate my loss? Wearing black allowed me to make physical the sorrow I felt so keenly inside.

I distinctly remember the day that fall when I put away the summer clothes for autumn. The days were becoming cooler, and short sleeves—even for my boys—weren't warm enough. Three months of black had narrowed my wardrobe, and I cried as I put away the T-shirts I'd stopped wearing after Rob died. Over the last months they'd been pushed to the back of the bureau drawers. I hardly remembered I'd owned them. It was as though they were from a different life, one that was now painfully gone.

After the funeral is over and the lengthy work of grieving begins, many bereaved people wonder, "Does anybody even know I'm still grieving?" This is where outward signifiers of loss can offer important guidance for those who love us as well as personal expressions of our grief. Whether you choose to wear black or engage in a social media fast, wear a torn piece of clothing as in Jewish tradition or shave your head as in Old Testament times, I encourage you to find ways to make physical the loss you feel inside. Get creative about how you manifest grief's presence in your life.

Sorrow so often defies words, and it may help to find ways to signify your pain that don't require speaking. The many practical dimensions of your loss will require you to explain your loved one's death over and over again. Articulating this to strangers can be particularly difficult. As you do this hard work, outward signifiers can offer personal solace as well as clear communication that you are a person who needs tenderness and compassion.

DO I HAVE TO DO THIS ALONE?

One of the greatest challenges of grief comes when we realize we must shoulder our sorrow alongside life's other responsibilities. We'll talk about managing the emotions of loss in the next chapter, and I do that on purpose. For most of us, the crash course of grief requires that we deal with nuts and bolts before we allow ourselves much emotional space to grieve. If you had only your own life with which to be concerned, that would be one thing. But you've now been tasked with closing down the life of your loved one. Finances, belongings, even laundry require your attention.

Perhaps you're what grief researchers call an "instrumental griever." You grieve by doing. After a death, there's sure to be a lot to do. You want to pour yourself into the task of honoring your person by resolving his finances or planning for the holidays, but you don't know where to start. The to-do list looks like it runs on forever. Or maybe you're an "intuitive griever," ready to let the practical tasks pile up as you process your feelings aloud.

Regardless of what grief expressions come naturally, most likely you'll appreciate a support team as you bushwhack through the forest of responsibilities that stands before you. The key to surviving the loneliness of grief is to not do it alone. As you walk this difficult path, you can assemble a team of faithful companions willing to walk with you—the Sam, Merry, and Pippin to your Frodo Baggins. These dear folks can't carry the heavy weight of loss for you, but they can encourage you and offer relief. They can become indispensable support because of their generous willingness to befriend your companion grief too.

The key to surviving the loneliness of grief is to not do it alone. As you walk this difficult path, you can assemble a team of faithful companions willing to walk with you.

Those who support you won't be perfect. They'll mess up or say the wrong things. Honestly, you will too. You're learning as you go just as they are. It will take time, but you can locate people who are ready to accompany you through this hard season and cheer you on as you aim your feet toward flourishing. Like the friends who climbed onto the roof to lower their friend to meet Jesus, this empathetic team will remind you of Jesus' presence in your pain and carry you before him through their care and prayer.

HOW DO I FIND THESE PEOPLE?

Just at the time you're meeting the new you, you need to navigate your relationships as well. I want to affirm just how hard this work can be. In each relationship after a loss, you meet as though for the first time but with baggage and history awkwardly attached. If you are fellow grievers of the same person, you each grieve your own unique relationships with that person. The similarities you hoped for may not be there.

All relationships change after loss. A close friend may now

never pick up the phone to call. A loved one may make painful remarks. It's hard to watch your loved one's death ripple out into other relational deaths. Take the time and space to grieve this, too. Listen to Job as he laments these changes in his own life:

> He has put my brothers far from me,
>> and those who knew me are wholly estranged from me.
> My relatives have failed me,
>> my close friends have forgotten me.
> The guests in my house and my maidservants count me as
>> a stranger;
>> I have become a foreigner in their eyes.
> I call to my servant, but he gives me no answer;
>> I must plead with him with my mouth for mercy.
> My breath is strange to my wife,
>> and I am a stench to the children of my own mother.
> JOB 19:13-17, ESV

Sound familiar?

You may find these shifting relationships confusing, frustrating, or irritating. Some people in your life will leave because they can't accept the new you. Others won't be able to see past your person's death to the person you are becoming post-loss. Death makes some things easier and many things harder. When relationships grow hard, it may be necessary to create new boundaries to maintain them. Sometimes you'll need to gently release a relationship altogether. Not everyone will be able to walk with you on this difficult path.

However, the arrival of grief in your life doesn't only have this negative effect. Brotherhood and sisterhood are often forged out of sorrow. In the miraculous kindness of God, you will also discover that "faithful are the wounds of a friend." Kind people will show up in unexpected places. Dear friends will emerge. As the writer of Proverbs puts it, in your grief you will find companions who are "born for a time of adversity." Grief does not just destroy relationships; it galvanizes them. Watch for these opportunities and celebrate them when they come. As you experience these changes, be sure to give space for new things to grow. If one is silver and the other gold, you'll benefit from both new and old relationships as you walk with grief toward new life.

WHO'S ON MY TEAM?

When I began preparing my tax return the first year after Rob died, I anticipated I'd need a little extra time. It was the last return I would be "married, filing jointly," and I wasn't sure what to expect. For almost twenty years I'd done our taxes, and I loved the job. So, on that evening when the kids were happily occupied playing, I sat down to create order out of my manila folder of papers.

I completed my taxes that night, and I went to bed feeling pretty good about myself. If everything else in my life was changing, at least this could stay the same. I could still file my taxes myself.

Except I couldn't. For the first time in almost twenty years, unbeknownst to me, I made an error.

A couple of months later, I was settling some financial

Grief does not just

destroy relationships;

it galvanizes them.

Watch for these

opportunities and celebrate

them when they come.

matters, and a question arose about my taxes. I sent along my completed return to a local accountant who told me politely but straightforwardly that my return was incorrect. He reassured me that taxes involving a deceased person were complex for the average person to file alone. I appreciated his kindness, but his comments were a blow to my ego. More than that, they hurt my heart. In this task where I'd once felt capable, I now needed to ask for help. I didn't want to have to admit that even in the mundanity of taxes Rob's death had wrought change.

For months I'd heard "How can I help?" or "Let me know what I can do for you," but I'd subconsciously resisted. Not because I didn't feel I needed help. To the contrary. My life had exploded into a million pieces with Rob's death; I knew clearly how devastated everything was. However, to accept help was to acknowledge that Rob's absence touched every part of my life—from grocery shopping to finances, from carpooling to plans for my future. My heart broke again each time I encountered a new place my loss touched. To hear someone offer help wrote that loss in cement. I didn't want to believe my life had radically shifted, but everyone outside my life could see it too.

It took me a little while, but I began to see that accountant as part of my post-loss team. Faced with the reality that there were certain areas of my life I could no longer navigate the same way, I knew I needed to assemble a group of people who would walk beside me and help me figure out the many practical dimensions of my loss. The amazing thing was this: when I became willing to look for people, I began to see them everywhere.

Like an NFL coach preparing for the draft, you'll find your-self scouting for helpers in the days ahead. You'll build a team of sorts, friends and acquaintances who will help you as you navigate all of the ways your person is gone. That day I began to build my team. Here's what I learned.

WHAT'S YOUR SKILL?

A few months into my loss, I sat in my grief counselor's office downtrodden. I'd recently talked on the phone with a friend who seemed to dismiss my grief. Her response had taken me aback. I'd laid out my heart, and she'd promptly changed the subject. I was bewildered. What was I to make of this?

As I talked through the situation, I came to realize that I'd asked my friend to be present in a way that wasn't within her gifting. She was a "get it done" type of person, not a feelings person. I'd hoped for connection, and she had seen a problem to be solved. Her response wasn't unkind or insensitive. She had simply responded with her gifts. If I felt rebuffed, perhaps it was because I had asked the carpenter to install the plumb-ing, so to speak. I'd asked her to function in a way she wasn't skilled to do.

First Peter 4:10 paints a beautiful picture of how family life works within the church and how, I believe, your team can work beside you in grief. The apostle Peter writes, "Each of you should use whatever gift you have received to serve others, as faithful stewards of God's grace in its various forms." Different people have different skills, Peter says, and all of them convey God's love and grace. Over time, I discovered that my friend would be indispensable to me on my grief journey. She'd offer wisdom and guidance when I was wrestling with a decision. When I honored her gifting, she flourished as a companion in my sorrow.

When you're ready to receive care and help, consider the people you love and who love you. What are they good at? Where are their skills? And how does their gifting align with your needs? Perhaps you wouldn't ask your accountant to bring you dinner, but you can definitely expect him to assist you at tax time. Your brother who becomes flustered with details nonetheless can provide a sensitive, caring ear when you need to release your sadness.

Grab a piece of paper and write some of these names down. Identify each person's skills and gifts. You're on your way to developing your own unique support system! Be sure to cast your net wide. Your list may have some unusual characters, but that's okay. This is all part of the growth that happens after loss as you learn afresh how to advocate for yourself in the world without your person. Notice a need in your life? A new friend might be waiting in the wings when you ask for practical help.

Over the three years since Rob's death, my support team has included family and friends as well as unlikely heroes like my electrician, my financial adviser, my realtor, and my HVAC guy. Your team will surround you with care and support, and you will be able to lean on them as other relationships shift and fade in the days and years after your loss. Some will remain in your life for this season, and others will become dear friends who last a lifetime.

HOW CAN I HELP?

"Let me know if there's anything I can do." No doubt you've heard that statement often since your person died. After a loss, many volunteer to assist but few show up for the job. I don't think this is because they don't have good intentions. On the contrary. Loss touches something in our common humanity that prompts us to reach out. But just because we experience empathy, that doesn't mean we know what to do with it.

As you identify people in your life who will walk with you through grief, put them to work! Household roles may have changed for you, and you could use assistance in lots of areas of your life. When you feel overwhelmed doing a task, that's a good sign that you may need a helping hand. Write down what makes you feel overwhelmed. Then, either hand the task off to a member of your team or find a friend who can walk beside you as you do the hard thing yourself. If you're overwhelmed but not sure what you need, ask, *How do I feel?* Then look beyond the feeling to the need that stands behind it.

Many people use meal trains to coordinate dinners for grieving families. If you're invited to accept a string of meals, go ahead and add practical needs to the list as well. Laundry, cleaning, lawn mowing, snow removal, and even grocery shopping can be a gift you receive from someone who wants to help in your time of need. If you don't need meals, ask a friend to develop a list of handymen or important people to call when needed. It'll save you the time of searching online for a plumber when you're in a grief fog. Enlist people who want to help but aren't sure how. As you offer practical opportunities, you will discover your team enlarges naturally. Creating simple lists like these are great ways to gently engage your brain without tasking it with higher-level orders like decision making.

Even as your team comes around you to offer care, some tasks may be so personal you want or need to do them alone. For example, many widows have shared with me that the financial concerns relating to their partner's death required their primary attention but felt intensely private. Opening the books of someone else's life can be such a delicate endeavor. Sometimes family members learn hard truths when they begin going through their loved one's papers.

As grateful as you are for the community who supports you, you will discover the push and pull for presence and privacy after your loss. These desires do not compete against each other; both are totally normal responses to the death of a loved one. You can create healthy new boundaries that allow for the connection as well as the space you need to make tough decisions, whether you must settle your loved one's estate, make decisions about her belongings, or determine how to spend holidays.

In cases where you desire to (or must) fulfill a responsibility alone, lean on a friend for emotional support. Briefly share with them the task before you and ask for prayer. Going into a hard meeting or fulfilling a difficult assignment can grow easier when we know a companion has committed to bring us before Jesus. For the prayer warriors on your team, your request will mobilize them to care for you the very best way they can.

WHAT ABOUT HIS STUFF?

After Rob died, I came home and boxed up his things. His baseball hats and clothes. The papers on his home office desk. In my shock and acute grief, it was just too painful to look at them every day. Rows of boxes all labeled "Rob" in black Sharpie lined the back of my bedroom closet, a quiet testimony to my heartbreaking loss. A whole life reduced to a row of cardboard boxes. Some family and friends offered to help me go through his belongings, but I just wasn't ready.

It's normal in grief to get rid of your loved one's belongings. It's also normal to hold on to them, sometimes for a very long time. There is no right or wrong, no prescribed way to say good-bye. As I neared the first anniversary of Rob's death, I slowly began the process of opening those boxes again, sifting through the memories inside, and figuring out what to do. Even three years later, it continues to be a one step forward, two steps back kind of process that requires sensing when to lean into my grief and knowing when I need relief.

There is no timeline or set of guidelines for how or when you need to deal with your loved one's belongings. Wait until you're ready, and do what feels natural to you. Research shows that grieving people benefit most from token remembrances of their loved ones. Many struggle when they rely on their person's belongings as a living link to what is lost.

This distinction is unique for each person. I can't tell you what defines remembrance and what becomes an unhealthy grasping for the past. As you turn to your grief, listen to its longings and fears. I trust that you will know. You may reflect your loved one's generosity by giving items away. You may find new uses for his or her things to honor the rebirth you are experiencing after loss. In this hard task, you can express the bond of love that continues even after death.

Abbie reflects on her mother's death:

We are sitting on the floor of sweet Momma's closet, surrounded by her clothes. Momma embodied beauty and grace in every way, including her impeccable fashion choices, always brimming with personality and possibility. But she is no longer here to wear her clothes. They sit untouched. Uninhabited, so to speak.

Momma told us what was to be done. "Wear them or donate them," she said. She didn't want her things to become unused or sit idle. But how do we take such a jarring step into the reality that she is never going to wear these clothes again? How do we bring ourselves to donate a lifetime of memories?

We take a deep breath and step into the closet together. We charge the darkness, welcoming both tears and laughter. "Remember when she wore this jacket?" "Oh my goodness, have you seen this one? How did she look so good in this!" We hold hands and give hugs. As we place the donations in bags, the empty hangers are what get me. Hundreds of empty hangers. I am completely undone. Sobs finally take over.

In truth, Momma was right. Her things should be used. Life needs to be lived. So we tell stories. We relive memories. We grieve what could have been. We dream of the days yet to be. We hope to look half as fashionable as our sweet Momma along the way.

WILL I EVER CELEBRATE AGAIN?

Like your loved one's belongings, holidays are infused with memory. After your person dies, it's normal to wonder, *Will I ever celebrate again?* Rob died just a week before our seventeenth wedding anniversary. A month later, our daughter turned fourteen.

The next six months felt like a gauntlet of holidays—Rob's birthday, Thanksgiving, Christmas, my birthday, Valentine's Day. I longed for a month without any holidays at all!

"Will I ever celebrate again?" is an all-or-nothing question, which I try to avoid in grief. So let's rephrase that to "How will I celebrate?" Death changes the shape of our celebrations, adding bitterness to the sweet. However, holidays and special occasions also bring perspective. They offer us vital doses of hope in the midst of despair. For the Christian, every moment of joy is, as C. S. Lewis said, a reflection of the greater joys that lie ahead of us. Grieving people desperately need these reminders.

The first holidays after your loved one dies offer new opportunities to grieve and honor your loss. To make a holiday easier, release your expectations for how it will play out. Anticipatory grief most likely will make the days before the holiday worse than the event itself. Remember, if you can forecast misery, you also are capable of forecasting joy. Even with grief at the holiday table, you still have agency.

If the holiday bird causes annual stress, maybe this isn't the year for a big turkey. As you release your expectations and open yourself up to new possibilities, consider breaking with tradition. The Ghost of Christmas Past may bring a festive air to a Dickens story, but you can't conjure up the past by rehearsing old activities. Determine how you will honor your person by looking back but also by looking forward. And, most important, by looking at the *now*. The first holidays after a loss may be times for reflection and sorrow, but, as Black grief counselor Rev. Arlene Churn writes, "These are meant to be celebrations—not another funeral."

Finally, if you decide to opt out of celebrations—your birthday, your anniversary, their birthday, Christmas—that's okay too. Grief attends each special occasion with you, and you get to determine what you and grief can handle together. If you're invited to a celebration and feel ambivalent about attending, offer a maybe. Accept invitations from family and friends who will understand if you need to back out or make a last-minute decision. Just as there is no one right way to address your loved one's belongings, there's no one right way to celebrate after they are gone.

Remember, if you can forecast misery, you also are capable of forecasting joy.

WHAT WILL I DO?

Wouldn't it be great if today were all there was, if we didn't need to think about tomorrow and the next day and the next without our person? I've often craved the shortsightedness I enjoyed in early grief. I was in such a fog, it never occurred to me that for *the rest of my life* I'd live without Rob. I'm not sure when it began to dawn on me that he was really, truly never coming back, that all of the tomorrows we'd planned for had been erased. That I needed to create a brand-new plan for my future.

There comes a time in your journey with grief when it hits you. You've hiked over the first rise of shock and disbelief and you see the path ahead of you that winds endlessly on toward the horizon. You have been called to walk with sorrow and suffering not just today but for all the days ahead. Grief will be there through every point on your timeline. *What will you do?*

Of all the practical dimensions of loss, this one will require the most of your energy and emotion. It is easy to become over-whelmed by the years that stretch out before you, so take your time. It will be a lifelong endeavor to acknowledge the reality of rebuilding a future without your person.

After your loved one dies, you may need to change many parts of your future—vacations, your work, retirement plans, college, or marriage. Many people will advise you not to make big decisions in the first year after loss, but I encourage you to beware of sweeping advice like this. Particularly if you have been a caregiver or seen death advancing, anticipatory grief plays a role in how you assess your readiness to make decisions after loss. Likewise, for those who have experienced sudden loss, decision making may take longer as you cope with the dramatic change in your life. Throw out the year mark and write your own future.

I'm a big fan of developing hierarchies to guide me in deci-sion making, and I encourage you to do this as you start to make practical decisions related to your future. When you're ready, clarify your top three or four priorities right now. Let your plans and goals flow out of those present priorities. Do you need to find a job, hire a nanny, ask for housekeeping help? Create a hierarchy (a fancy word for a list in prioritizing order) as a way of dealing with the things that are hardest for you in grief. Work on the easiest first!

As you adjust to your loss, this method will give you space to address pressing needs first and table bigger issues until you have more emotional bandwidth or new knowledge to offer insight into your decision making. Hold your plans loosely, allowing yourself margin to change your mind as you grow and change in your loss. Above all, don't feel pressure to make long-range decisions. As hard as it is to believe right now, the future will truly take care of itself.

PRESENT IN SUFFERING

God's good plans for you did not die with your loved one. Take a moment and read that again, out loud. After so much sorrow, I know that this is a major act of trust. I know how hard this is; I live it every day alongside you.

However, if we are told by the apostle Paul that we do not grieve as those who are hopeless, it is here—in the nitty-gritty of everyday practical matters—that we can see the first rays of hope emerge from the darkness of our loss. From the people who surround us with support to the tasks we complete that become acts of honoring our person, all of these manifest love that persists after loss. All point us to the God whose faithful love pursues us even in the depths of sorrow and suffering.

Jesus is deeply interested in the minutiae of your life. He knew about the marital history of the woman at the well. He made sure every mouth was fed at the feeding of the five thousand. He cares about the phone call you had with the lawyer, the boxes that need packing, the life that needs rebuilding. As you navigate each practical dimension of your loss, grief and God walk with you together. He has cared for the sparrow and the lily, and he will care for you, too.

FOR YOUR OWN REFLECTION

1. What are some physical, external ways you could signify that you are grieving? List three that you could try.

2. Support comes in a variety of ways. Draw three concentric circles and make an X for yourself in the middle. List your most intimate support people in the center circle. List your second tier of support in the next circle. Finally, write the names of supportive acquaintances in the outer circle. Review their names and think of the skills and insights they offer to your life. Determine whom you can call on to support you in particular ways that showcase their gifts and contribute directly to your needs.

3. Have you gone through your loved one's things since his or her death? If so, how did that make you feel? What did you decide to give away or keep, and why? If not, what holds you back from starting this process? What do you need before you can approach it?

4. Choose a particular holiday and list how that day is different now that your person is gone. Now, write a list of how that day remains the same. What insights does this activity offer you as you reshape your expectations for this day?

5. Throughout the Gospels, we see Jesus concerned with the intimate needs of those around him. How can you invite Jesus into the practical dimensions of your loss? How does his companionship bring solace as you walk beside grief through these hard, everyday matters?

CHAPTER 6

On the Shores of Loneliness: Wading through the Emotions of Loss

My lyre is tuned to mourning, and my pipe to the sound of wailing.

JOB 30:31

I'm a baseball mom, and after my two boys, Pigpen—the third baseman on Charlie Brown's team—is my favorite player. He's friendly and easygoing—and perpetually surrounded by a swirling cloud of dirt and dust. His cloud is such a part of him, in fact, that on the few occasions when he arrives without it, nobody recognizes him anymore! Try as Pigpen might, he can't permanently shake the dust off his feet. That cloud almost has a mind of its own. You might say the cloud of dust is Pigpen's companion.

In all my searching for metaphors that describe our emotional experience with grief, I can't think of one better than Pigpen's cloud. Swirling, vision obscuring, hard to shake—yeah, sure sounds like grief. Grief arrives and, like Pigpen's cloud of dust and dirt, its presence becomes a defining part of our identity.

Most of the other Peanuts characters mock Pigpen for his cloud companion. They avoid him, tell him he's filthy, encourage him to try harder. Even Pigpen tries to get rid of his dirt a time or two. But here's the amazing thing. Along the way, Pigpen comes to accept his cloud companion. He proudly describes it as "the dust of countless ages." More than that, he finds true friendship in Charlie Brown, the one person who isn't intimidated or repulsed by the unseemliness of his situation.

When most people talk about grief, they refer to the emotional dimensions of loss. But if you haven't lost someone close to you, you may not realize how big grief actually is, how hard it is to unearth yourself from the mess its presence makes in your life. Grief is stomach upsets and sleepless nights. Grief is paperwork and probate court and estate sales, what author Wendy Gan calls "the bureaucracy of death."

In, among, and over all these day-to-day struggles, each of us walks around with our own swirl of emotions. We're a lot like Pigpen. In grief, we may be short of patience or cry at the drop of a hat. We go silent in conversation or just can't handle noise. Often, like Pigpen, we discover a painful truth: this cloud of emotions repulses other people. While any number of emotional expressions can be a normal, natural part of the grief experience, we're left alone to navigate with grief swirling around us, clouding our vision.

WHY WALKING WITH GRIEF IS SO HARD

In 1969, Elisabeth Kübler-Ross identified what is now popularly known as the "five stages of grief"—denial, anger, bargaining, depression, acceptance—as she studied and interacted with individuals who had received a terminal illness diagnosis. As a person came to terms with his diagnosis, Kübler-Ross asserted, he would move from denial to eventual acceptance before his death. Though it was never scientifically proven (and actually was disproved in subsequent research), the model became a popular one.

The "five stages of grief" were intended originally to describe the emotional trajectory of a dying person, not those they left behind. Because of the popularity of this linear model, many grieving people (and those who try to support them) find themselves totally lost when they encounter the emotional dimension of their grief. We're expecting a road map, and what we get instead is a Pigpen-style dust swirl.

If you've tried to chart your emotions from one day to the next, you would be hard pressed to find a clear trajectory in the days that follow loss. Instead, your drawing would probably look more like Pigpen's cloud. We've been taught one thing about grief, but we live something different. No wonder we're confused!

As you continue your journey with grief, you'll want to spend time engaging with the emotions grief provokes. Resilient people face their loss, not avoid it. Because your emotions are a gift from God, you can trust you'll find him here, even when everything swirls around you, even when a way forward is hard to see.

FEARFULLY AND WONDERFULLY MADE

Grief isn't just a passing feeling. It is an emotion and a capacity that God wove into our bodies at birth; it is part of the marvelous divine design of emotional range. God built into us the ability to love, forgive, hope, and, yes, grieve.

When grief arrives, it can feel like a real roller coaster of ups and downs. We find we're able to get through a day without crippling sorrow only to be surprised a few weeks later when we're steamrolled by sadness. A get-together with friends sounds appealing on Monday only to loom intimidatingly on Friday night. We think we've adjusted to the emotions of loss, only to find we're thrown for a loop as the fog wears away and we realize we're experiencing something new, with few tools to address the questions we face.

> God created all our emotions, and he called them good. Our emotions bear witness to the parts of our souls that cannot be easily accessed with the intellect, to those places within that speak truth with primal honesty.

As Christians, we often believe that our intellect and reason can be trusted but our emotions cannot. We defend our minds and dismiss our feelings, warning ourselves and others that "feelings come and go." We become nervous about making decisions based on emotional impulses, as though God cannot speak wisdom in these intangible parts of our psyche.

Furthermore, we often categorize our emotions as good or bad. Love, compassion, and courage are positive and to be commended. Anger, jealousy, and grief are negative and should be avoided. But God created all our emotions—anger, love, even jealousy and grief—and he called them good. Emotions are just as much part of the magnificence of our *imago Dei* as are our reasoning skills. Our emotions bear witness to the parts of our souls that cannot be easily accessed with the intellect, to those places within that speak truth with primal honesty. As my sister so aptly told me after Rob's death, "Your gut is indwelt by the Holy Spirit too."

When sin twists our emotions, we should name these distortions as wrong and pray that God would redeem them. The apostle Paul makes this distinction when he tells the Ephesian church, "In your anger do not sin." Anger may be an appropriate response, but sin is never okay. As we study the Gospels, we see Jesus express the whole range of human emotions, from righteous anger to selfless love to honest grief. Over and over, God blesses our emotional range by exhibiting his marvelous design perfected in Jesus. Grief, then, is not inherently bad. It need not be fixed, only managed in spiritually, physically, relationally, and emotionally healthy ways.

NOBODY LIKE YOU

As little girls, my sisters and I sat every afternoon before the television to watch *Mister Rogers' Neighborhood*. With that blissful gentleness that wooed children for decades, Mr. Rogers smiled serenely at the camera and crooned, "There's only one like you. Nobody else. Nobody else. Nobody else but you." If I could tell you only one thing about your emotions in grief, I'd sing you that song over and over. When it comes to the emotions you experience after your loss, there's only one like you.

Emotional expression is unique to each person. Research

confirms that there are no masculine or feminine ways to grieve; there's just you and the way *you* grieve. Some people are what psychologists call "intuitive grievers." They feel most comfortable when they express their emotions outwardly through crying or talking. Other people experience more "instrumental" grief; they think about their loss but don't say much. They work out their grief in constructive activities in a hobby or sport or art form.

Our emotions are a gift to help us cope with the changes in our lives, and all of us will probably express our grief in instrumental and intuitive ways at one time or another. Expressing your grief is natural and normal; it isn't a sign that you need therapy or that you can't cope. Rather, by expressing grief in healthy ways, you actually ease the burden of walking with it. Therefore, your most important work as you face the emotional dimensions of your loss is to simply learn what grief expressions feel most comfortable to you.

THE VALUE OF CRYING

After Rob died, a friend confessed to me, "I don't know whether to talk about Rob with you or not. I don't want to make it worse. I don't want to make you cry." I appreciated the sensitivity to my emotional state, but the concern was misdirected. My grief would have been far worse if I'd had to bottle up my feelings.

We sing, "Big girls don't cry." And we tell our sons, "Real men don't cry." Our culture exhorts us to shoulder through or man up. Tears in public are generally seen as a sign you can't hold it together. At the graveside we tell each other, "He

When You Need Extra Help

If trauma is part of your loss, you may find that you need extra help to listen to your emotions. Your body was beautifully designed to handle stress, but trauma causes unique challenges. You may want to navigate these in the care of a professional who has walked this road with many others like you. If trauma, anxiety, or depression is part of your story, reach out to your family doctor or a mental health professional. There's a big difference between grief and mental illness. After losing your person, you deserve the best care to help you find flourishing again.

If you experience suicidal feelings or ideation, connect 24/7 with the National Suicide Hotline at 800-273-8255. Don't feel ashamed to call. They're used to talking to people experiencing grief. Grief can make life feel really dark, but you don't have to let the darkness overcome you.

wouldn't want you to be sad," and we dry our tears and try to move on. We avoid mentioning the person who died because we don't want to make it worse. (How much worse could it be? He's dead!) We bottle up our emotions, assuming that stuffing them away will make them go away.

This kind of emotional constipation does a number on our ability to process our grief. Hiding the hurt never helps. When we tell ourselves that our loved ones wouldn't want us to be sad, we minimize the intimacy of those relationships. What husband wouldn't want his wife to be sad that he was no longer with her? It simply doesn't make sense. When we avoid making our grief public, we cut ourselves off from sources of support and encouragement. But our avoidance of crying doesn't just do a number on our emotional state. It isn't good for our bodies, either.

Before we talk about why crying is a valuable part of the grief experience, I need to clarify. God wired each of us uniquely, and crying isn't a natural part of every person's emotional range. I married a man who teared up only a handful of times in our almost twenty years of marriage. As I reflect on my own life, I can't think of a single time I wept in public before Rob died. I teared up at preschool graduations and sad movies, but nothing about my emotional makeup indicated I'd wail in parking lots and sob in church when my husband passed away.

When we talk about the benefits of crying in grief, we must do it while keeping an eye on those myths about grief we discussed in chapter 2. Because they are often outwardly manifested, emotional expressions in grief can easily become codified. After all the work we've done to dismantle those unhelpful myths, I don't want to build them back up again here! The ways you express your grief are uniquely yours. They need not be determined or directed by cultural expectations about crying or not crying. However, as you express your loss in your body, you need to know that the fullness of emotional expression is available to you, whether or not you choose to use it. I hope you'll explore that range at least once as you get to know your companion grief. Here's why.

For hundreds of years, popular belief has told us that you'll feel better after a "good cry." Enthusiastic social scientists have attempted to make connections between the chemical makeup of emotional tears and physiological benefit. But the truth is, we don't really know exactly how crying benefits the body. We do know a few things though. Crying tends to lower our heart rate and can slow breathing, two stress-relief indicators. Crying can exhaust our bodies, driving us to rest. Because it is an outward expression, crying can indicate to others that we need care, offering us vital emotional connection. Sometimes you feel worse after weeping: your head aches and you're worn out. Other times, you feel a release. Whatever has weighed on you is now off your chest.

While science still has much to learn about crying, it may be a grief expression you find helpful as you process the absence of your loved one. And if you never shed a tear, don't worry that you're not normal. Don't feel pressured to do what doesn't feel natural. You and grief have an intimate relationship now, and you can choose to express that relationship in a way that feels comfortable to you.

GRIEF ISN'T JUST SADNESS

My grandmother Betty offered herself in selfless love to my grandfather, her beloved Hans, in the latter years of his life. Parkinson's and Alzheimer's slowly ate away at the man she had once known so intimately. His dying was a long, sad goodbye.

When death finally arrived, Betty was exhausted and ready for rest. Though she grieved her husband deeply, she also was relieved. She, too, had fought the good fight and finished her caregiving course. It had been a hard and painful honor to fulfill her marriage vows to the end.

Grief isn't as simple and uncomplicated as plain old sadness. Whether your relationship with your person was close or complex, your loss sudden or anticipated, you'll likely experience a diverse range of emotional responses as you walk with grief. After loss, all of our emotions are filtered through the lens of our loved one's death. If you've been a caregiver like Betty was, you may have experienced anticipatory grief during caregiving and discover you're relieved or feel set free after the funeral is over. If your relationship had grown thin with your loved one over the years, you may experience regret or disappointment.

Grief isn't as simple and uncomplicated as plain old sadness. Whether your relationship with your person was close or complex, your loss sudden or anticipated, you'll likely experience a diverse range of emotional responses as you walk with grief.

As you encounter these various emotions, you can learn to meet all of these feelings with compassion and understanding as natural parts of the grief experience. You can learn when and how to share your emotions in ways that bring relief and health as well as strengthen relationships with those who support you. You can learn how to give grief a voice and shape its narrative.

I spent almost fifteen years teaching in settings varying from homeschool classes to college seminars. While I was enthusiastic about my subject, I learned quickly that classroom management would be a significant part of my job. To successfully run a classroom, I needed to engage students in conversation and moderate that conversation as it grew over the course of a class period. When it comes to engaging your emotions in grief, I think a classroom is the perfect visual picture to help you see how the various feelings you experience fit together.

Imagine a classroom inside you. Your emotions—anger, disappointment, hope, joy, and more—sit in rows or around the conference table, and they all have something to say. If your relationship with your person was fraught with conflict, perhaps frustration speaks loudest. She talks without raising her hand. She sometimes loses her cool at unexpected moments. She has valid things to say, but she often dominates the conversation. Or perhaps you're feeling your loss so deeply that you have no words. Loneliness sits in the front row of the classroom of your heart with her head on her desk. Throughout the day, she sits in the same position, quietly weeping into her hands.

Take a moment and imagine your own heart's classroom. Who is sitting in the front row? Who demands to be heard? Who can barely lift a hand to answer when called upon? Who barges in after class has started and drops his books on the ground in a huff while plunking down in the back row?

Every good teacher will tell you that each voice in the classroom is important. It is the honor and responsibility of an educator to encourage the quiet voices, amplify the unheard ones, and moderate the loud and consistent talkers. The most dynamic conversations happen in a classroom when everyone participates. There's a beautiful synergy that occurs when individual voices come together, teaching and learning from one another. Just as it happens in a great classroom, this can happen for you in grief.

I want you to know that all the emotions you experience in grief are normal and can contribute constructively to processing your loss. In fact, I believe we need all our emotions to be able to acknowledge our loss fully. Often the emotions that we stuff away or hold back are the ones that offer us the most wisdom

Don reflects on his son's death:

My wife and I lost our only son, and oldest child, at age 21. Just weeks after Ian's death, we attended the staff Christmas party of the big church where I served on staff. An icebreaker started the evening off, where we each wrote on our name tag a current emotion we were feeling "during this Christmas season." We were to then walk around the room and share that emotion with two other people.

Just to play along, I wrote "Peace." My wife tapped me on the shoulder. I turned and saw the name tag stuck to her sweater. It read "Bereaved." Under the word was a smiley face and a Christmas tree. I burst out laughing. Everyone in the room turned toward us. The senior pastor said, "Hey, you two, you're having way too much fun, and our Christmas party has barely started."

Pulling the name tag off her sweater, my wife replaced it with another one on which she had written "Hopeful." Her first name tag was just for me, and it did exactly what my wife intended—gave me a good laugh. In our deep sorrow, grief and joy inexplicably lived together. We learned to embrace them both and live with the mystery.

when we turn with compassion and listen. As you encounter the emotional dimensions of your loss, this will be your great challenge and honor—to receive your emotions as a gift from God and allow them to help you integrate your loss into the person you are becoming. You can adjust to grief's companionship by inviting all of your emotions to inform your life. If you need support, invite a trusted friend or grief counselor to listen beside you.

BOUNCING BACK AND FORTH

As psychologists Margaret Stroebe and Henk Schut studied bereavement, they noted the nonlinear nature of emotional responses people had after losing their loved ones. Ditching the image of a road map moving from denial to acceptance, Stroebe and Schut developed the Dual Process Model, a Venn-diagram theory of coping, to describe what they thought showed a better picture of how grief actually behaves. As we cope with loss, Stroebe and Schut said, we bounce back and forth between loss-oriented emotions and restoration-oriented ones. Sometimes our emotions allow us to process all that is gone. Other times they draw us forward into our lives after loss.

Christians have read, prayed, and sung this dual model of processing for millennia as we have studied the Psalms. Forty-two songs of lament appear in the Psalms, all with this loss and restoration focus. In biblical lament we hold together accusation and trust, sorrow and praise. In these psalms we see that God welcomes us to share everything we feel, even when our emotions aren't scrubbed up clean and dressed in their Sunday best. Even better, our emotions don't need to follow a smooth trajectory from despair to hope. The number of lament psalms alone tells us that this is a dual process we'll engage for the rest of our lives. The back-and-forth you feel in grief is reflected in Scripture. It's a normal part of the spiritual journey.

Whether you use the lament psalms as your guide or you imagine your heart's classroom filled with many voices, the intention is the same. Healthy emotional processing requires us to engage all the emotions that need to find their voice and invite God to be present in the conversation. When you experience joy, grief may twinge and remind you of your loss. You may rage and despair and rejoice all in the space of one twenty-four-hour period. A mother who lost her daughter in a drunk driving accident channeled her frustrations into restoration-oriented activity as she founded MADD, Mothers Against Drunk Driving.

Remember that leaning in and letting go we talked about in chapter 4? You'll want to apply that same wisdom here. Understanding that you're always bouncing back and forth between loss- and restoration-oriented coping, you can step to the front of your heart's classroom and take charge. Let's dig a little deeper here and look at fear as an example.

LISTENING TO FEAR

A brush with death almost always provokes fear of some kind. If your loved one died suddenly, you may struggle with catastrophic thinking. *What bad thing will happen next?* If you watched your person's life slowly ebb away, you may harbor fears about your own health, about your life now without him or her. You may bottle up your grief out of fear of being emotionally overwhelmed. Fear may reveal itself in your life choices after loss, your eating habits, or your relationships. Death is a scary thing, and it's a normal human response to feel afraid.

After Rob died, I wrestled with fear in a variety of ways. I feared dying and leaving my kids parentless. I poured out to God how afraid I was to lead my family without my husband, how frightened I felt about instantly becoming the breadwinner for my kids. My fears were all reasonable; life had upended, and everything felt helter-skelter. Fear was a student in my heart's classroom, standing on the desk, waving her arms in the air, and

If leaning into our emotions

means listening to them,

letting go requires knowing

when they've had enough

air time or aren't accurately

describing the situation.

shouting, "Help me! Help me!" If I was going to find a healthy way to walk with grief, I'd need to figure out how to address this loud voice in my life.

Silencing that voice wouldn't make things better, so I began to turn to my fear with compassion and a listening ear. What I discovered surprised me. When I listened, fear revealed my distrust of the world and my insecurities about myself. Fear showed me how black-and-white my thinking often became in times of crisis. Even though I trusted God's goodness and power in my life, fear regularly drew my eyes, like Peter's, away from Jesus beckoning me forward and onto the swirling waters below me.

As I tuned my ear to fear's voice, I began to hear it echo behind other voices in my life. The anger I felt? That was "fear, brought to the boil," to borrow journalist Caitlin Moran's phrase. The loneliness I sometimes thought would drown me? That was fear too—fear of becoming insignificant, fear of being unloved, fear of being forgotten. By engaging my loss-oriented moments of fear, I actually could understand my grief better.

If leaning into our emotions means listening to them, letting go requires knowing when they've had enough airtime or aren't accurately describing the situation. Sometimes when my grief's fear spoke, I noticed it got off track, and I learned I needed to speak up. Was I actually unlovable because no one had called me that day? Was I really unsafe when I lived in a quiet country town with neighbors who looked out for each other? Should I really approach God with suspicion when he'd faithfully carried me thus far?

As I became accustomed to attending to my emotions, I discovered I could naturally oscillate from loss to restoration.

It was okay to sometimes ask fear politely to take a seat. It had contributed enough to the conversation, thank you very much, and now it was time for a breather. I didn't need to force a smile or push through the hard moments. I could feel them fully, then let the emotion crest and ebb away naturally into a moment of more levity. I could offer my fears to Jesus, knowing that he was sufficient to care for me.

Fear wasn't always a loss-oriented emotion for me though. Sometimes it propelled me forward to restorative activity. My fears about my future led me to complete a graduate certificate in nonprofit management, a career field I'd left a few years before. I found new confidence in knowing my skills were once again up to date should I need them. My fears of loneliness compelled me out of my natural introversion to develop new relationships. I discovered new friends in places I hadn't expected them and strengthened old friendships even across miles. Listening to fear sometimes offered me needed motivation to try to live again.

My story isn't that different from yours. I suspect that fear stands behind many of the emotions you experience after loss, waiting to talk. Maybe fear isn't the loudest voice in your heart's classroom. Perhaps it's anger or loneliness or resentment. Whatever that voice is, I encourage you to listen. Your grief has important things to say. As you allow Jesus to reveal these to you in your sorrow, you'll notice you can flow between loss and restorative emotions with more acceptance.

OTHER VOICES IN THE CLASSROOM

Myriad stressors bear down on us after our loved one dies, and moments of levity can offer light or—to our surprise—additional weight. When you understand that leaning in and letting go are the normal rhythm of grief, you can release even the guilt and shame you might feel in those moments and instead live them fully. Life with grief will always carry a bittersweetness for you now. Your son's loud, happy birthday party will have you laughing and misty-eyed at the same time as you think of his sibling who isn't there. Your dinner table banter will both invigorate and quiet you as you remember the voice that used to rise above the rest or interject a timely joke.

Joy doesn't cancel sorrow. We know this for sure. But we also must acknowledge that it works the other way too. Sorrow doesn't cancel joy. Your life after loss embraces this mystery of our miraculous design—we are capable of complex emotional engagement. Just as you turn a listening ear to fear or anger or disappointment, be sure to listen for hope and joy. Allow these, too, to speak in your heart's classroom.

When my oldest daughter began looking at colleges, I encouraged her to look for a campus that focused on diversity and gender balance in its student population. Having attended seminary where I was often the only female in the room, I knew how important it was to have a variety of voices represented. My graduate experience had been richer because of students from Asia, Africa, and South America who sat beside me in the classroom, and I wanted my daughter to remember how ethnic diversity and gender balance could offer her a broader and more well-rounded educational environment.

I'll offer you the same advice, dear reader, when it comes to engaging your emotions in loss. Feel the sorrow deeply. Express the despair, the doubt, the anger, the exhaustion. And when you catch your breath, take a deep inhale of hope. Listen for the quiet whisper of possibility. Drink deeply the rich words of joy that Scripture offers you, not in isolation of your suffering but in its presence. Explore the full emotional range God has given you to express your grief. As you listen to grief and her attending sorrows, let courage, hope, and bravery speak too.

FOR YOUR OWN REFLECTION

1. How does it make you feel to know that your capacity for grief is a God-given design?

2. Does crying help you? Why or why not?

3. Draw your own Venn diagram of loss- and restoration-oriented emotions and activities. What fits in each category? How does visualizing your grief in this way help you to accept the frequent shifts you experience emotionally?

4. Name five fears you have related to your grief. Remember to look behind other emotions for the fear that might be hiding there.

5. How can retracing your steps offer you hope as you move forward in your life after loss?

CHAPTER 7

Dark Nights beneath the Stars: Searching for Spiritual Answers to Loss

[It is not] that I am (I think) in much danger of ceasing to believe in God. The real danger is of coming to believe such dreadful things about Him. The conclusion I dread is not "So there's no God after all," but "So this is what God's really like. Deceive yourself no longer."

C.S. LEWIS, *A GRIEF OBSERVED*

Naomi stood and traced circles in the dirt with her foot. Deep lines marked her weathered face. She kicked at the dusty soil again and raised her eyes. How many times had she rehearsed this scene after her husband, Elimelech, had died? How many times had she woken in the night to remind herself that one death could not cause another? And yet, here she was again, graveside, mourning two sons gone too soon.

After Elimelech had died, Naomi had grieved deeply. For so many years, he had been her security, her home away from home in this foreign land. She grieved their years in Bethlehem before the famine drove them out. She grieved the journey that had brought them far from family, the miles that now separated her from the comfort of her homeland. She wept as she remembered the lifetime of ordinary moments they had shared as partners creating a new life in a new place. Even as they had longed for the Judean hills again, Elimelech and Naomi had come to love their new home in Moab. This foreign place was woven into all their memories of their boys' childhood years.

Naomi leaned more heavily on her sons after Elimelech died. Mahlon and Kilion both had loved her well as she mourned. They each carried their own sorrow, and together the three mourned Elimelech with an intimacy that only they could understand. His death bound their hearts together, and that bond upheld Naomi on her darkest days.

With her sons and their wives, Ruth and Orpah, Naomi had constructed a new life—a widow's life—filled with new people and new activities, together with a grief that never shrank in size, even as her new life grew around it. The years crawled by at first. Each festival, each month a painful marker of Elimelech's absence. *He should have been here*, Naomi would recall with sadness as each celebration and each harvest came and went.

But slowly, almost imperceptibly, her life began to open. Hope shone on the horizon. Elimelech was gone, but Naomi saw that life could and must go on. Her sons loved her dearly; her daughters-in-law embraced her with kindness. In the shelter of their love, she could start again. The sorrow that had marked those early years after Elimelech's death was beginning to feel less acute. Perhaps God would shine his face on her again.

But just as she'd begun to trust—this horror. Not one but *two* sons gone. Only a decade since she'd stood in this place before. Now her sons lay beneath the soil beside their father. Her whole family—her whole life—buried, dead. After Elimelech died, Naomi had pleaded with the Lord. *You took him from me, but do not take my children.* Perhaps God had not heard her cries. Perhaps he had other plans. Perhaps he simply didn't care.

Bitterness began to swell in her heart. *How could this happen? Elimelech, and now Mahlon and Kilion, too.* Where was God? No traces remained of this life they had built together against the rolling hills of Moab. The sun that warmed her back reminded her of her thirst, an irony not lost on her. No earthly draft could satisfy her parched heart now. *Better call me Mara,* she thought wryly. *The filled-with-bitter-water one.*

NAOMI, A GUIDE IN GRIEF

Since your person died, I wonder if you've felt like Naomi. Gutted. Overwhelmed. Trampled by life's sorrows. Have you wondered if God *does* give you more than you can handle? Have you questioned whether he is good or even if he exists? Have you longed for the life and for the God you knew before? If so, Naomi's the woman for you.

There are myriad characters in Scripture to whom we could turn for a discussion of the spiritual dimensions of loss. Job suffers in righteousness, and Hannah waits sorrowfully but patiently. But Naomi travels her grief journey with far less finesse. That's precisely why I like her. When your theological arguments are exhausted and your patience turns to anxious urgency, you need a woman like Naomi to tell it like it is. When it comes to searching for spiritual answers, Naomi makes an excellent guide in grief.

In the four short chapters of the book of Ruth, we meet a

woman completely undone with sorrow. Naomi makes absolutely no bones about how she feels about God and what she feels he's done to her. She feels abandoned and unheard, and she says it—not just in her head but to her friends. Presumably, to anyone who will listen.

If we're honest, we've felt that way more than once since grief became our companion. Whether we have followed Jesus for years or death has prompted us for the first time to explore his claims, we all have wondered where God is in all of this. When I connect with grieving people, over and over again they tell me that God feels far away. God seems silent. Sometimes, I'll be honest, I don't know what to say. I have felt that way too, and I know that no one's sorrow is assuaged by offering chapter and verse to affirm a truth that doesn't dull sadness or wipe doubt away.

That's why I appreciate Naomi. She sheds light on the places we are afraid to admit exist in our spiritual lives, even in the darkness of sorrow. Many Christians feel they cannot grieve because they believe in heaven and the hope that comes from being united with their lost loved one after death. They worry about getting too close to sadness, despair, and anger—"negative" feelings they've been taught Christians should avoid. Just as our culture uses platitudes to lessen the shock of death, we often twist or simplify spiritual truths in an attempt to offer the same comfort. We say things like,

- "Rejoice. She's in heaven."
- "This was all part of God's plan."
- "God must have something better for you."
- "God must have needed an angel."

All of these ring hollow. Why? Because they're simply not truth—oversimplified at best, entirely heretical at worst. Our heavenbound loved ones can and should be grieved. Even for the most faithful believers, God's plans will remain shrouded in mystery. His intentions are not a Rube Goldberg machine of chain reactions. And nobody—read that, *nobody*—turns into an angel when they die. These are dangerously twisted spiritual truths, and their Hallmark-card sentiments don't hold us up. Thankfully, there's something better.

Just as God wrote Naomi's story, he is writing yours and mine. The honesty with which she faces her loss, her wrestling and doubt and discouragement—these are all a natural part of what it looks like to lose someone we love. Even when you believe that God's Word is true and faithful, death really hurts. And here's the best part. God doesn't love us any less for our doubts in his goodness. He doesn't lose his patience when our questions drag on and on. He doesn't get offended by our anger. We see in Naomi's story that God does not withhold future happiness because we struggle to hold to his promises in the depths of our sorrow. God's promises to Naomi—and yes, to you and me—remain true and faithful even when we feel like our worlds have exploded.

GOOD CHRISTIANS GET SAD

A few weeks after Rob died, a well-meaning stranger sent me a note that said simply, "God is your husband now." No doubt, her words were meant to encourage me. Nevertheless, hands down, it was the hardest spiritual truth I received in that tender season. I didn't want God. I wanted *Rob*. Or, better phrased, I wanted God *and* Rob. As Elisabeth Elliot said of Jim's death, "God's presence with me was not Jim's presence. . . . God's presence did not change the terrible fact that I was a widow."

From Old Testament narratives like Naomi's to psalms of lament, to Jesus at the cross, the Bible welcomes us to sit at the intersection of sorrow and faith. Nevertheless, we often believe that good Christians, when confronted with trials, sing joyfully with nary a care. When faced with loss, good Christians pivot easily from their earthly beloveds to the arms of the Bridegroom himself. We sing, "Why should I feel discouraged? Why should the shadows come? . . . His eye is on the sparrow, and I know he watches me." And we cloak our very human longings in a spiritual shroud meant to bury them deep inside us.

> Good Christians get sad. Good Christians weep, mourn, lament, and wail. Good Christians doubt and get angry. We don't need to show up in our Sunday best when our lives feel crushed. We can live the full range of emotions before God in honesty and trust.

I want to tell you plainly and simply: Good Christians get sad. Good Christians weep, mourn, lament, and wail. Good Christians doubt and get angry. We don't need to show up in our Sunday best when our lives feel crushed. We can live the full range of emotions before God in honesty and trust. Even more glorious, our questions, our doubts, our anger, and our frustration can become our holy offering to God, our testimony of commitment to him even when we question what he's doing in our suffering.

Does this need to look polished and graceful? Absolutely

not. Psalm 55:22 invites us to "cast [our] cares on the LORD," but the picture the original Hebrew paints here isn't a calming Monet. The word *cast* literally means to fling, to hurl. When you're suffering, God doesn't invite you to Sunday-morning decorum but to a veritable Jackson Pollock action-painting mess. Burdened by disappointment with God? Fling it on him. Wrestling with spiritual questions you can't answer? Hurl them at him. Psalm 55:22 invites you to throw God everything you've got—your misery, your loneliness, your sense of abandonment—with this astounding promise: "he will sustain you." He will nourish you. When your paint pots of misery finally run dry and your frustrated strength melts into exhausted sorrow, God will still be there, ready to offer you everything you need.

Still not sure? Let's sit down with Naomi and see how all of this intersects with her faith. What do you do when the one you had trusted to carry you feels dreadfully absent in your pain?

WRESTLING WITH GOD

Naomi does four important things in the book of Ruth that I'm convinced will be helpful to you as you encounter your own wrestlings with God: she keeps the line of spiritual communication open, she laments, she listens in the silence, and she steps forward in faithfulness. With grief as her companion, Naomi finds her way to renewed faith and purpose. I believe you can do this too.

Naomi's path to flourishing begins the way all healthy relationships start—with open, honest communication. Naomi minces no words about how she feels as she looks at the wreckage

Jackie reflects on her husband's death:

Control seemed to be a theme that was threaded through my grief journey, which began with my husband's cancer diagnosis in 2004 and followed for the next seven and a half years. My sorrow was not just anticipating the end of life, but grieving dreams, travels, and family while still caring for my husband. This year would have been our fiftieth wedding anniversary, so it is a time to reflect and realign where God is directing me.

Letting go is not something I do well. I have always treasured people and possessions. Passionately. Thinking they were mine to care for and love. My husband's stage IV brain cancer diagnosis reminded me no matter how much I loved or cared for him, God had ordained his days and mine. Staring this death sentence in the face, I realized I need to hold the people and things of this world lightly, for they are so temporal. I need to hold tight to God's hand and to his promises, for they are eternal.

of her life. She feels abandoned by God, and she isn't afraid to say it out loud. "The Lord's hand has turned against me!" she proclaims in frustration. Upon arriving home to Bethlehem, her old friends excitedly rush up to greet her. How does Naomi receive their welcome? "The Almighty has made my life very bitter," she cries. What a sad hello.

Naomi's wrestling with God, no doubt, makes her friends uncomfortable. None of their spiritual platitudes seem to work anymore. To their "God will make a way," Naomi grumbles, "The Lord has brought me back empty." To their "God never gives us more than we can handle," Naomi shouts, "The

Almighty has brought misfortune upon me." All of this from the woman who had specifically returned to Bethlehem because she'd heard God was on the move there! She'd returned to the House of Bread, where God was feeding in the midst of famine. *Surely he will feed me, too*, she thought. And yet she had the gall to say out loud that he'd given her short shrift!

We can flip ahead to the end of the story and see that Naomi makes eventual peace with God. But in this moment, the truth of Naomi's deep loss and the reality of her deep faith are revealed. In her acute grief, she feels abandoned by the God she'd loved and followed, and she knows he is big enough to handle her anger and frustration and despair.

When it comes to wrestling with spiritual questions in grief, follow Naomi's lead and keep the lines of communication open. Talk to God even if you don't feel like he's there—*especially* if you think he's not there. You don't need to have happy or hopeful words. You just need to have honest words. "A broken spirit, a broken heart . . . God will not despise that offering if that's all you have to offer." If you can, find a friend who will commit to talking to God with or alongside you. Let them know you're having trouble, and ask them to lift you up to the God you're wondering still cares.

GET IT ALL OUT

A dear friend and I used to go out to dinner once a month when we were young moms. While our husbands watched the kids, we sat over wine and delicious Italian food and chatted till the restaurant closed. Often at our favorite spot, my friend would send her meal back to the kitchen after it arrived at our table.

The food was cold or the chef hadn't made the dish gluten-free per her request. She wanted them to get it right.

Compliant and conflict-avoidant as I am, I initially thought her requests were kind of rude. While she was always polite and gracious, I didn't think it was okay to complain. At all. Eat the cold dinner, and don't go back again. But ask the chef to right the wrong? That didn't sit well in my stomach.

Over the years and many dinners together, I realized that *I* was the one who had it wrong. My friend was lavish in her praise of a fine meal, and she was committed to the flourishing of others. She heaped praise on her favorite local eateries and frequented them faithfully. She talked to the waitstaff and cooks with the congeniality and knowledge of a food critic and super fan. She had worked in event planning and food service, and she knew restaurants operated on a thin profit margin. Most couldn't afford to serve a bad meal. Her complaints about cold food weren't meant to cut anybody down. Her lament about a poor meal actually showed she cared about the restaurant's success.

If you read the book of Ruth, you may start to feel like Naomi is a real Negative Nellie—until you understand the function of biblical lament. Mark Vroegop writes, "Lament is the language of a people who believe in God's sovereignty but live in a world with tragedy. . . . Part of the reason it's hard is that they believe the promises in the Scripture. They are fighting to trust in those promises through the tears." Our complaints—the life we want to send back for a redo in God's kitchen—can function as acts of trust.

As you commit to keeping the lines of communication open, feel free to get it all out. Complain like Naomi. Ask God for a different meal—no more tears as your food day and night, but a life where grain and new wine abound. Tell him your frustrations and fears. Explain all the ways your hopes and dreams feel crushed. Ask him all the questions you long to have answered.

Christians often feel like these questions are off limits or reveal a weakness in faith. After the loss of a loved one, many people wrestle with the nature of sin and evil or the problem of pain. You may question the character of God or the possibility of life after death. Even if you've been walking with Jesus for many years, this is totally normal after an encounter with death. Christians regularly experience eschatological distress in the face of loss. You may wonder if heaven is for real, if you'll ever be happy again, or if God is really good. As you wrestle with your faith in the face of your loss, tell God how hard this is for you.

LISTEN IN THE SILENCE

I once visited a high-end restaurant in Vancouver, British Columbia, where video screens were installed in individual bathroom stalls. Once you latched the door behind you, the screen booted up and began to play. It felt like the perfect motherhood cliché. Even in the bathroom I couldn't get a sliver of silence.

We North Americans hate silence. Screens talk to us in restaurants, in airport terminals, in the grocery store checkout lane. It is no wonder, then, that we don't like it when we perceive God as quiet, especially when life is hard. Oftentimes in grief and in crisis, we crave words, assurances that we are not alone, that the end of suffering is near. We cry out, "How long,

O Lord?" We demand, "Why do you hide yourself in times of trouble?" And we expect an answer. We want God to speak.

Our desires are partly warranted. God is at his essence a communicator. He spoke creation into existence, sent Jesus as the Word made flesh, and wrote his message to humankind in sixty-six books. He has promised to hear us when we pray, and throughout Scripture and church history he has responded to the cries of his people. Dallas Willard writes in his classic *Hearing God*, "People are meant to live in an ongoing conversation with God, speaking and being spoken to." But how do we live when it appears Jesus has nothing to say? Could it be that there are moments when something more than words is needed?

While Naomi doesn't doubt God's existence (that would have been incomprehensible in ancient times), she does think he's cruel and vindictive. She complains, "The LORD's hand has turned against me." God's punched me in the gut. He's dealt me a crushing blow. When you feel like that, no words will reason you out of that position. You need something more.

In the book of Job, God eventually quiets Job's questions with a stream of "Where were you?" questions that display his majesty. However, scour the book of Ruth, and you'll notice God never answers Naomi's complaints with words. He never presents an argument to show her how faulty her faith has been. He never chastises her for being weak or overly angry. Instead, in the silence, God offers Naomi comfort of a different sort, the kind she can receive when her mind is swirling with questions and her heart is shrouded in doubt and sorrow. God gives Naomi the same kind of care her great-great-grandson wrote about in Psalm 23. God answers in the silence.

THE LOVE BEHIND THE WORDS

In Psalm 23, we never read of Jesus speaking. We run to these verses in times of trial and sorrow—straight into the arms of a Shepherd who doesn't have any lines to say. Of course, we know that shepherding was not a silent job. Elsewhere in Scripture we read of Jesus the Shepherd calling his sheep by name. He tells us in the Gospel of John that his sheep know the sound of his voice. Verbal communication is foundational to our relationship with our shepherd.

But verbal communication isn't the only way that Jesus communicates with his sheep. As I used to tell my public speaking students, verbal communication isn't the only way to talk. Our bodies often speak more powerfully than our words ever could. I suspect we know this intuitively when we run to Psalm 23 in times of pain. There are some places too dark and heavy for words. There are places where another kind of communication is most needed.

In Psalm 23, the psalmist describes an affectionate, protective, loving shepherd's actions. Jesus leads us beside still waters, prepares a table for us, comforts us with his rod and staff—nonverbal gestures that tell us just as much about his care as his words do. Jesus never has a memorable line, but his actions speak volumes. He gives us what we need in our hour of struggle: his strong and quiet provision and presence.

As Naomi wrestled with her disappointment with God, God spoke in the silence. He provided fruitful work for Ruth. He orchestrated a relationship with Boaz. God gave and gave and gave again without ever saying a word. After Ruth came home overflowing with grain from the fields she'd gleaned, Naomi

Instead of the words we want, in silence God offers us his quiet presence and asks us to trust him. Perhaps he knows more words do not always bring peace. Only his presence can do that.

could see it as plain as the nose on her face. "[The LORD] has not stopped showing his kindness," she said, "to the living and the dead."

Whoa. Just one chapter earlier, Naomi bemoaned her emptiness. She wailed at the misfortune she believed God had brought upon her life. Where was God? The same place he'd been all the time. Providing for her, speaking to her. And when she could not hear his voice, he was speaking through actions, not words.

We love words because we love the Word himself. But God may not offer you words in the midst of your loss. He may never clearly answer your questions in a way that satisfies. As we sit, like Naomi, in the silence of lament and sorrow, we can learn to seek and embrace the Jesus who comes to us between the words, the Jesus who appears in times of trouble to be awfully quiet. This Jesus is no less capable when he does not speak. He is no less attentive to our needs. Naomi and Psalm 23 remind us that his care simply takes a different shape. He knows our every need and fulfills it, even if he does not say a word. We can trust our Shepherd even when we do not hear his voice.

Dallas Willard writes, "No matter how well we know his voice, words from God will not spare us times of grief and pain, as Jesus was not spared." Many times, we demand words of divine reassurance but hear none. But lest we read God's silence as inattention, Naomi and Psalm 23 reassure us that he is still communicating. There is not a moment when we are out of his mind or forgotten. He always gives us exactly the kind of care we need. Instead of the words we want, in silence God offers us his quiet presence and asks us to trust him. Perhaps he knows more words do not always bring peace. Only his presence can do that. So he offers us his strength in silence, the arms of a Shepherd surrounding us when words fail.

STEP FORWARD IN FAITHFULNESS

The book of Ruth closes with a scene that's worthy of a Hollywood tearjerker. In the last verses, the writer paints a beautiful tableau of Naomi holding baby Obed in her arms. Her friends, those women who had greeted her when she first returned to town, gather like clucking hens around the new chick. "Naomi has a son!" they coo as they gaze at the darling child. If you remember the woman we met in chapter one, you might think you'd fallen down Alice in Wonderland's rabbit hole. Curiouser and curiouser, indeed!

How did Naomi get here? What happened to this woman who had questioned God's goodness, his provision, and his presence? What questions had been answered for her to arrive at this beautiful moment? Did she simply have a short memory or disregard the pain she had endured?

I have no doubt that when Naomi held that baby in her arms, she thought of Mahlon and Kilion. As her daughter-in-law Ruth lovingly looked on, Naomi probably glanced up and thought about what might have been. This baby she held in her arms would bear no resemblance to her son, the man who had died without fathering a child. What God was giving her after loss was something entirely new. Had God proven himself faithful over time, despite her distrust, anger, and unbelief? Yes. Had God answered her questions? We're never really told.

I look back over the last chapters of Ruth to discern Naomi's path, and I see a winding road from misery to mystery. Walking with grief as her companion, Naomi plodded along. She sent Ruth to the fields to glean daily. She helped her snag Boaz's attention. She explained to Ruth the social rituals that would secure her future. She carried her longings and her ache and her questions along with her as she did the everyday tasks that life required. Naomi stepped forward in faithfulness.

When grief takes up residence in your life, you may encounter myriad questions for God. Your anger and doubts may loom large. But as you wrestle with God, lament, and listen in the silence, you can still step forward in faithfulness, even when you don't have the answers you want to hear.

Three hundred years after the book of Ruth was written, Israel's prophet Isaiah penned these words:

> The children born during your bereavement
>   will yet say in your hearing,
> "This place is too small for us;
>   give us more space to live in."
> Then you will say in your heart,
>   "Who bore me these?
> I was bereaved and barren;
>   I was exiled and rejected.
>   Who brought these up?
> I was left all alone,
>   but these—where have they come from?"

ISAIAH 49:20-21

I sometimes wonder if Naomi marveled in a similar way at the provision God had brought out of her sorrow. Isaiah's words remind me that even when we don't understand his plan, God is still working. In our grief, he is quietly birthing new life that will someday fill us with its abundance. And one day, when we look back in wonder and ask, "Who bore me these?" the only answer will be Jesus. We were bereaved, exiled, left all alone. We couldn't trace his hand, couldn't see what his plan was in all of this. But he knew what he was doing all along. He was working for our good.

FOR YOUR OWN REFLECTION

1. How has your experience with grief and faith been similar to or different from Naomi's?

2. Before your loss, did you believe that sadness, doubt, or anger toward God represented a lack of faith? How has your person's death changed or reinforced that view?

3. What questions do you have for God? Write a list of them, and then commit to praying through them for a week. How does bringing your questions intentionally and directly to God shift how you perceive his attention and presence in your pain?

4. Do you feel like God has been silent to your cries? How might Psalm 23's picture of the Good Shepherd invite you into a larger view of what God is doing in your life?

5. Hebrews 11:1 tells us that "faith is confidence in what we hope for and assurance about what we do not see." How does this verse speak to your walk with grief today? How can you step forward in faithfulness, whether or not God feels close today?

CHAPTER 8

And a Little Child Shall Lead Them: Parenting through Loss

Just as he lived with them alive, he will live with them dead. Someday he will accept their death as part of his life. He will weep no more. He will carry them in his memory and his thoughts. His flesh and blood are part of them. So long as he is alive, they, too, will live in him.

PEARL S. BUCK, *THE BIG WAVE*

It is no exaggeration to say that parenting my children through loss has been the most challenging task I have ever faced. At the time of Rob's death, my children were ages 7, 10, 12, and 14. My youngest had celebrated her birthday only a month and a half before. Six months later, I blogged these words in my online journal:

> I want to tell you what it feels like to hold a child as
> he mourns. I want you to know how it feels as his
> body, wracked with sobs, sinks deep against your own.
> You hold his tender frame, cradling him in your arms
> like when you soothed him as a baby. The maternal

instinct that prompted you to rock him all those years ago returns, and you begin to gently sway, rubbing his back, breathing deeply of his scent to ground yourself so that you are not swept away in the deluge of his grief. He shakes with the weeping, stops to grab a breath, and then returns to sobs. His hands grasp your body like he's afraid of drowning. Every fiber of his being laments.

No more powerless feeling exists in all the world than to see your child endure a pain you cannot take away, that you cannot assuage even a bit. There exists no distraction, no reward, no encouragement, no gift, no friendship that can fill the aching void that compels him to tears. Death has pierced his tender life, and sorrow now has darkened every part. Behind every smile he hides a broken heart.

Even I—the one who bore the blow before him, the one who held him as he heard the news—even I cannot temper that pain. As close as we are, I still feel the impotent onlooker. I bear my own burden of sorrow, but I cannot bear his, too. His sorrow is intimately his own, even as I walk beside him through it.

I hold my fatherless child in my arms, and my tears wet his hair. Together we weep. I pray that in his sorrow he will never sense divine abandonment. Like Jacob wrestling with God, I demand a blessing on this tender boy whose spirit is crushed with longing for the father he has lost. I rock him, and I beg his Maker for mercy. Lord, have mercy. Christ, have mercy. Mercy for this broken one. This courageous little grieving one. And mercy for me, too. The mother who promises to hold him close until his weeping gives way to tired sleep.

As a widow, I have been required to shoulder my own grief while helping my children learn to carry theirs. It has been an exhausting, beautiful, heartbreaking privilege. With children spanning early elementary, junior high, and high school years, my first few years after loss have been a crash course not only in child development but in grief and trauma development as well.

Even when they experience a shared family loss like that of a grandparent, parent, or sibling, children express their loss in ways that are unique to their developmental stage and personal wiring.

Children grieve differently than adults do. Even when they experience a shared family loss like that of a grandparent, parent, or sibling, children express their loss in ways that are unique to their developmental stage and personal wiring. Their bereavement reflects their growing sense of self and their understanding of the world. They process their loss at each new stage of maturity.

Research estimates that approximately one in fourteen children lose a parent before the age of eighteen. Five percent of children lose a sibling during childhood. Chances are, if you are grieving, there is a child within your relational sphere who is grieving too. If you work with children as a teacher, troop leader, or Sunday school teacher, statistics tell us you regularly interact with a child who is processing loss. Whether you are parenting or leading a child through loss or you're simply trying to understand your own childhood or inner longings, this chapter is for you.

For many years, children's grief was largely overlooked and understudied. Cultural presumptions of the past were that children who passed through emotional fires either dug deep into stores of inner resilience or became wayward—not much in between. Children who suffered loss became presidents or prisoners. Thankfully, our understanding today is much more nuanced. Organizations like the Dougy Center for grieving children and families and the National Alliance for Children's Grief and studies like the landmark CDC-Kaiser Permanente Adverse Childhood Experiences (ACE) Study now offer us insight and tools to walk with children and encourage them toward flourishing. Their journey with grief's companionship—like our own—need not be a wandering in the dark. Children can learn to grieve well too.

CALLED UP TO THE BIG LEAGUES

Almost ten months after Rob died, we began our first baseball season without him. Quarantine because of the COVID-19 pandemic had closed all of our town's fields, and weeds took up residence all over the warning track, in the bullpens, and in the dugouts. When we arrived for practice, the place was a mess!

One night the kids and I spent an hour weeding the bullpen to get it ready for games to start. As we sat in the gravel pulling up renegade plants, the commuter train whistled into town. I looked up. By instinct. I didn't even think. I heard the screeching wheels, and my body knew. He was coming home from work.

Except that he wasn't. Never again. I could look up every time I heard that train screech to a stop, and I would never see Rob jogging across the parking lot, his collar open and suit jacket over his arm, rushing to make it to baseball practice on time, not wanting to miss his boy's opening pitch for that evening's game. Baseball seasons would come and go, and Rob would not see any more of them.

When I think of how children grieve, I can't help but think of the many hours I've spent at the Little League field over the years and the way children's engagement with the game changes through their growing years. The death of a loved one calls children up to the big leagues, so to speak. For most children, facing their person's death will be the biggest challenge they've encountered in their short lives thus far. Let's explore this analogy a little more.

LITTLE CHILDREN AND GRIEF

When my children first started playing ball, their coaches (many times Rob himself) tried to nail down the fundamentals. *This is the ball. The ball goes in the glove. We run the bases counterclockwise. When the ball is pitched, we swing.* The information felt incredibly simplistic and elementary until a preschooler asked you how many quarters were left in the game or why the "referee" wore blue, not black and white. A child who sat glued to the screen watching the Red Sox play the Yankees could never hope to go pro if he couldn't find his way to his own team's dugout or remember that the official was actually called an umpire.

In those early years, baseball often felt like babysitting or herding cats. The complexities of the game were clearly a lot for little minds to comprehend.

When it comes to the complexities of death, young children's understanding isn't all that different. Their understanding evolves over time as their capacity for intellectual engagement grows. I remember the first time my daughter asked me what it meant to be cremated. Barely seven years old when her father died, she had a lot of concrete questions, not unlike the child's question about the umpire's outfit. She'd heard the word mentioned, but I'd not explained it to her. She simply wanted to know the facts.

For young children (age six and under) experiencing loss, death primarily means absence, if it means anything at all. Toddlers and young children may not notice a loved one's death, or they may perceive the absence as imaginary or impermanent. Furthermore, object permanence—the understanding that if something vanishes from view, it still exists—is a significant developmental milestone for babies. We celebrate when we can leave the room and they don't cry or when we can drop them off at preschool and they don't worry we've abandoned them. Therefore, it stands to reason that when a loved one dies, young children struggle to grasp what that absence means. In their first years, we've reinforced over and over again the exact opposite.

To wrap their little minds around the big concept of death, many young children ask the first four of the classic journalistic questions—*who*, *what*, *when*, and *where*. They may want to know what their loved one looked like when he or she died, what it feels like to be buried, or when their loved one is coming back. Like the kids on the ball field, they're trying to figure out the fundamentals of how this whole dying thing works.

Conceptually we can understand this as parents and caregivers, but our hearts are pierced when we need to field these sorts of questions. When you sense a child's fear that her grandpa can't breathe underground, it's easy to want to cushion the truth. But honest, forthright conversation about death is fundamental to a child's ability to grieve and grow in healthy ways.

> *If we're going to help the little ones in our care, we're going to need to help them face death with honest language to help them grasp the truth.*

If we're going to help the little ones in our care, we're going to need to help them face death with honest language to help them grasp the truth. Whenever possible, use real words that offer developmentally appropriate description to give your child clarity. For example, "Aunt Sarah died because her body was very sick." You can be honest and gentle at the same time by using basic language a small child can understand.

As you seek to be a helpful companion and guide for the children in your care, remember that the questions they ask should be answered with concrete words as much as possible, even questions you initially perceive as spiritual ones. For example, a question like "Where is he?" for a four-year-old is a concrete one, not an abstraction. As hard as it is to do, accompany your conversation about heaven with real, honest facts about where the body of the child's person actually is.

Take, for example, the little girl who said she wanted to

die so she could be with her dad again. Along the line, she'd heard that death was the gateway to eternity, and she figured that if she took the same path, her father would be waiting for her on the other side. A well-meaning discussion about heaven had given her complicated longings. Rather than muddy good theology about Jesus, angels, or God's goodness and sovereignty, try to keep these conversations separate from specific questions about the reality and process of physical death. At this age, few little children understand the difference. If you choose to say, "Grandpa is with Jesus," be sure to also say, "Grandpa is dead."

Because of their limited comprehension, young children may not appear to be grieving or may appear to "move on" quickly after loss. Less than forty-eight hours after my husband died, my youngest cheerfully asked to go to church with her friend on Sunday morning. Was she insensitive or uncaring? Definitely not. She simply didn't understand the depth and breadth of what had just occurred. At her age and in her shock, she couldn't comprehend that her daddy was never coming home again. Research confirms that "as children grow, they will need to re-experience the loss at each stage of development." What your child seems to miss or overlook now, no doubt, is registering and will reappear later on.

ELEMENTARY-AGE CHILDREN AND GRIEF

In the same routine I'd always kept when Rob was alive, one Sunday afternoon I announced to my kids that I was leaving to go grocery shopping. I told them I'd left the family cell phone on the kitchen counter and reminded them to call me if they needed anything. And then one of my children came in for a long, tight hug. And it hit me: my children understood that sometimes well-intentioned people leave and never return. They understood that death is real, that it is something to fear.

The elementary-age child (age seven to twelve) understands fear rooted in reality. While death still means absence, older children possess a clearer understanding of death being the cessation of life. They've had pets die. They've watched movies and television shows where parents are absent or death plays a thematic role. Their growing understanding of the world means that children understand finitude and physical pain. They understand that death can be scary.

Like little children, elementary-age kids often want concrete information to rebuild the story of loss. They understand that they can die, and they understand that the death of their person affects their own lives. Concrete questions help to orient their loss both within their inner emotional world as well as their outer world of everyday rhythms and activities. A child this age might want to know how a person develops cancer or where you'll go for Christmas now that Grandma is gone. All of these questions stem from a desire for stability and consolation of that fear that is a natural response to loss. Children want and need to know that, even in the face of death, they are going to be okay.

Therefore, your task as an adult companion is to help the child find that stability. This means committing to open communication—being available to answer questions about death and loss, being willing to admit when a question genuinely has no answer, and being honest about the ways grief will walk with them as they grow. After the loss of a loved one, create regular space in your home life to answer questions related to the death. Around the dinner table, shift from sharing nightly highs and lows to inviting conversation about the person who has died. Ask your child how she feels that day or if she thought of the loss during the normal rhythm of her day. Remember your commitment to use real language, not euphemisms, even as you point your children to eternal hope in Christ.

You may notice that your child displays what I call "popcorn grief"—grief that pops up and then seems to stop. He or she may experience very little grief during the day but have trouble with nighttime or tired moments in the afternoon. All may seem well one day only to have the next day be full of fear or frustration. It can feel like a real roller coaster sometimes! Your steady openness will offer them an anchor when emotions feel out of control.

Even when the loss is shared, our experience of it is not the same. It's important to remember that we need to avoid projecting our grief on children or, worse, pulling them into our grief. These kinds of behaviors can have lifelong consequences. Each child—like each adult—will experience bereavement that is unique to them.

Some children at this age will say little to nothing about their loss, and—hard as it is to believe—that's normal too. Art activities, building projects, musical expression, and sports participation can all offer children vital outlets for the emotions that they aren't sure how to articulate in words. School, social, and behavior disruptions are common grief responses for children at this age. Your committed attentiveness to your child's needs will go a long way in helping you notice and care for these issues. Enlist help from your school, church, family, and friends to build a web of support for your child. The mentality that "it takes a village to raise a child" makes a big impact on positioning your child for resilience.

TEENS AND GRIEF

Over the past three years since Rob's death, I have watched my children grieve and grow through major developmental changes. Three of my four children have become teenagers in these short years since their loss. What grief looked like the day their father died looks very different now.

Teenagers comprehend at adult levels the permanence and reality of death. They understand the effects of a death on their own lives. They can see how death plays out into the future. While teenagers may have *who, what, when, and where* questions about death, they often focus more heavily on the *why* questions that are harder to answer. As caregivers and companions, we are tasked with walking with them through the complex and often mysterious dimensions of wrestling with the emotional and spiritual questions they carry.

After a loss, you may find that your teenager tries to ignore death or becomes seemingly obsessed with it. Both are normal responses as these young adults try to orient death into their greater understanding of what it means to be human and what it means to live in a world touched by loss. Rumination is common, as are grief expressions in word and action. Behavior disruptions and developmental setbacks can also be within the range of normal.

A local school administrator once commented to parents

that children at this age wake up each morning to find themselves in a brand-new body. Adolescent changes really do seem to happen that fast sometimes! With so much physiologically changing, it's no wonder that in grief—as in life—most teenagers simply want to feel normal. As grief-aware parents and companions, we are already committed to normalizing grief, so this should be right in our ballpark! Your teenager can understand cultural lies about loss, and you can help shepherd him or her to avoid them.

The teen years are a challenge for even the most valiant parent, and grief in the teen years can be just plain hard. But learning to walk beside your teenager through loss can also offer an incredible bonding opportunity. All the things our teenagers may accuse us of—being heavy-handed, restrictive, or smarter-than-thou—don't ever work well in grief support. Loss levels the playing field. As you acknowledge this to your teen, you may find that he or she appreciates your honesty. She wasn't trying to get you to fix her problem anyways. She simply wanted you to listen.

WHAT CAN I DO?

Research clearly shows us that "bereaved children do not experience continual and intense emotional and behavioral grief reactions." Instead, they grieve and grow, grieve and grow. Shepherding a child through grief involves a delicate balance of offering both honest answers and space to simply be a child. Grief calls us to prepare our children for a world in which we cannot control outcomes. Sorrow reminds us that we must continually offer them to God's care.

Cathy reflects on her mother's death:

When my mother died, many friends expressed kind words about the hope of seeing her again. And while the hope for a future reunion brings comfort, it does not erase the longing that occurs as I wait.

Christians call this present time of waiting the already and the not-yet. Because of Christ's death and resurrection, we are already redeemed. But the suffering in our world reveals that the work of redemption is not yet complete. Christ has already conquered death, but loved ones still die, and we are left grieving.

Yet we do not grieve as those who have no hope. Hope does not ignore the brokenness. Paul writes, "Who hopes for what they already have?" Hope acknowledges what we do not yet have—restoration, healing, justice—but it also expresses confidence that Christ will come again to complete his work. When we live in hope, we participate in the redemptive work of the world. I eagerly anticipate when the not-yet becomes the now. But as I wait, I choose hope.

Because we know that children will grieve again at different developmental stages (what researchers call "re-grief"), we need a plan for engagement that will work from their youngest years until they're ready to leave the nest. Extensive research affirms that children are wired for resilience, but that kind of transformational growth doesn't just happen. It requires intentional investment from adults in children's lives who are willing to stick around for the long haul, infusing their relationships with gospel truth and Jesus' love. Let's consider how to do this.

THE FOUR L'S

Just two weeks before he died, Rob taught our youngest to swim underwater. On a hot summer night at a campground pool in Salt Lake City, she jumped off the deck into his waiting arms over and over again. Perhaps the thrill of jumping made her brave. When Rob asked if she wanted to try ducking her head underwater—something she had resisted for years—she said yes. I captured her big moment, and we all cheered. She's beaming in the picture I took. Years of failed swim lessons ended that night. Three years later, I can't keep her out of the pool.

Kids experience newness very differently than adults do. Sometimes they resist it with every fiber of their being. They defiantly hold their heads above the water and tell the instructor, "I *will not* put my face in." Other times they slip beneath the water with so much finesse you'd think they were born swimming. As parents, we cajole or threaten, encourage or stand back in silence. We feel we need to intervene in (or worse, control) the process. Many times, though, when encountering something new, our children simply need us to trust their innate wisdom. They'll do the new thing when they're ready. Engaging with children in grief is a similar task of waiting on their wisdom. We can facilitate healthy grief engagement and response by regularly practicing the four L's—listen, learn, love, and let go.

Listen

As you care for a grieving child, commit to a relationship of listening. When possible, let the child lead in conversation. If she doesn't want to talk, that's okay. If she does want to talk, be an active listener. Rather than asking your own questions, simply reflect back to the child what you think you've heard her say. Ask, "Did I get that right?" Her words are more important than your own. If the child asks questions that are hard for you to answer, graciously receive the questions and acknowledge your limits. If the question could be answered with some research, offer to look it up and get back to him or her with the answer. If you need help, a children's grief counselor can facilitate conversation further.

Learn

All children are impressed when they can teach an adult something new. Take the posture of a student when you engage with a grieving child. Sit at their feet and learn more than teach. First, assume the child understands his own emotions. As adults, we regularly operate under the assumption that we are older and wiser and know more about the world. But when it comes to feelings, each person is his or her own expert. If a child tells you he is happy, celebrate his happiness with him. Don't assume he's covering up deep sorrow. If he seems gloomy, let him describe his emotions to you without fear of judgment or interrogation. In either case, celebrate and commend the child for expressing how he feels. Second, accept your child's grief expression at face value. Help the child in your care find ways to express his or her loss in ways that already feel comfortable and natural.

Love

Isn't it obvious that grieving children need our love? It might seem that way, but it's amazing how easily distracted we can become with our own relationship to the deceased person when we share a common loss with a child. As you focus on loving your child, beware of turning him or her into a living icon of the lost loved one. Adults can be particularly prone to this danger when the mutual loss is a family member. The child may have his mother's eyes, his grandpa's wit, or his dad's shoulders, but he's still his own person. He may have received a quarter or half his DNA from his family member, but he's still uniquely himself. A child should never be used—overtly or inadvertently—as a living memorial to their lost loved one. Be careful not to search a child's face looking for your loved one instead. Children, just like adults, long to be seen and loved simply for who they are.

While some children appreciate comments that draw attention to traits they share with their deceased loved one, other children find these comparisons uncomfortable. If you're not sure whether your comment will be well-received, err on the side of caution and keep it to yourself. Or ask the child for her thoughts. "Would you like it if I shared with you some ways you're like your mom?" You might be surprised by what she tells you! Be sure to listen attentively and respond with her needs in mind, not your own.

If you've lost your spouse, the love your children need can sometimes feel like a burden on the already challenging task of parenting through loss. The popular airline adage works well here as you seek to love your children well within their loss: *Put on your oxygen mask first before assisting others beside you.* As you commit to self-care and self-love in your own grief process, you will discover that your bandwidth expands to care for those little ones God has placed so intentionally in your care.

Look for creative, time-saving ways to love yourself and them together. Your care for yourself in the midst of grief is itself an expression of love to your children. They need you more than ever, and by caring for yourself, you show them you want to be there for them in all the ways they need.

Let Go

Jesus told his disciples that unless they became like little children, they'd never inherit the Kingdom of God. For two millennia since, we've tried to pin down exactly what he meant. Did Jesus mean we needed the innocence of children, their willing trust, their joyful enthusiasm? What exactly is it that children offer in abundant supply? When I look at the way my children have navigated grief, I know at least one thing I want that they possess. I want their relentless pursuit of growth and new life.

Ask any little girl what she wants to be someday, and no doubt she'll give you a laundry list of ideas. She wants to be a princess, a barista at Starbucks, a mommy, a president. Nothing feels out of reach; no hope or dream too preposterous. Life stretches ahead, filled with possibility. Growth isn't just hoped for; it's expected.

As you companion children through grief, work hard to embrace this mindset. Expect and celebrate growth. Children's bones heal much more quickly than adults' do. It's nature's beautiful design. Kids have lots of growing left to do, and their bodies know it. In a similar way, children will move forward with their grief in ways that are very different from the adults around them. Their processing pace will look different. Their outward manifestations of loss will change as they age.

We look at our children
and muse, "They have so
much life left to live."
The truth is we do too.
When we engage with
children, we need to talk
and live like we believe this.

If a child no longer cries about a deceased loved one or talks about her, she may simply be moving forward with her grief in an age-appropriate way. You need not grieve this growth. The most damaging comments my children received repeatedly in their grief were centered on adults' grief-clouded vision-casting for their futures. Comments about "growing up without your dad" regularly conveyed only loss with no slivers of hope. They reflected an unfortunate adult tendency toward limiting "realism" and a resistance to resilience.

Our number one goal for our children after loss is that they would have a happy life, that grief would not crush them. We look at our children and muse, "They have so much life left to live." The truth is we do too. When we engage with children we need to talk and live like we believe this. We need to let go and release our children to lives of flourishing that await them even after all they have endured.

For children who suffer the loss of a loved one, maturity comes faster than for their peers. In painful ways they must grow up before their time. And yet this deeper understanding of the world can produce empathetic, resilient adults who contribute to their communities and build strong relationships with those they love. Just as it is for us, grief need not break our children.

In grief, our children seem so vulnerable. As they mourn, it feels like too much pain and sorrow for a little body to endure. And so it is with great relief that we can offer them to Jesus in their grief, the Good Shepherd who delights to carry little lambs on his shoulders to rest and safety. We can listen to, learn from, and love our children as they sorrow. And we can daily bring them to their heavenly Father, letting them go into his care, trusting his good plans for their futures.

FOR YOUR OWN REFLECTION

1. Do you have a story of loss from your own childhood? How did you respond to this death? How did the adults around you respond? What did their response teach you about grief?

2. Can you name a child you know who has experienced loss, whether the death of a loved one or another kind of loss (such as divorce)? Say a short prayer for that child now. Ask Jesus to carry this little lamb in his arms.

3. What can you do with your impulse to fix when you see a child in grief?

4. Is listening openly to a child hard for you? How might you cultivate the spiritual gift of listening as you interact with a child you know who is grieving?

5. Jesus tells us to come to him as little children. What does that mean when we read those words through the lens of grief? In your sorrow, how can you come to Jesus as a little child? What would that look like for you?

PART 3

THE

PATH

LEADS ON

CHAPTER 9

The Trail Ahead:
When Grief Is No Longer New

Mourning has its place but also its limits.

JOAN DIDION, *THE YEAR OF MAGICAL THINKING*

If you were an eagle flying two hours north from my home, you'd see a fascinating bit of geology from the sky. Here on the East Coast, far from the Pacific Ring of Fire, a small circle of mountains lies blanketed in sugar maples and pines, the remnants of an ancient volcanic caldera. Unlike its younger cousins to the west, the Ossipee mountain range in New Hampshire hasn't seen volcanic action in 125 million years, when the caldera collapsed into this remaining ring dike.

With trails accessible to the average hiker, the Ossipee range teems with visitors each summer. Few probably know that the ground they walk on used to be a volcano that would have rivaled Krakatoa, Vesuvius, or Mount Saint Helens. To most hikers, these mountains are just an afternoon of cardio, but from the sky you can see they're so much more. Even if you can't see it easily, Earth bears the scars. A volcano once was here.

It may be hard to believe, but eventually your grief will become like this. Hidden from view by life's new growth, overlooked by all but the most inquisitive, grief grows up and grows old. Just like that forgotten volcano, grief becomes part of the scenery, an integral and integrated part of our new landscape. Life grows around us, and we change and grow with it.

If your grief is still fresh and acute, it may be hard to envision this shift. Honestly, you may not even want to. Your gaze may be so focused on the past that you find it difficult to picture a future. It's hard enough to envision a future without your person, let alone believe that one day grief might not be all there is. Your feelings are real and valid. If you are there right now, take all the time it takes to feel your loss deeply, lament it loudly, and grieve fully. It's okay to feel the way you feel.

But in the midst of the weeping and gut-wrenching sorrow, as the days and months and years go by, I invite you to observe the changes happening within you and around you. How is grief's companionship shaping you? What nuances do you see that you didn't notice before? As time passes and grief becomes a familiar part of our life's landscape, we are called to a new, maturing relationship with our sorrow. When the agony of those first months and years wears down to a familiar ache, a dull pain, and a wistful goodbye, how exactly do we grieve with hope? What might it look like for our grief's topography to evolve like the Ossipee Mountains?

It is precisely when grief becomes an old, familiar friend that we are able to see this transformational work begin. You can thrive again after loss. Like a diamond made fiery bright through compression and heat, your life can shine with hope after the intensity of your loss as you integrate your grief. Like the Ossipee range, your woundedness can become the soil in which beauty can grow. In infinite wisdom, God has brought you to this new day. In gracious love, you are here. There is still purpose for you—good, beautiful, awe-inspiring purpose. God invites you to live fully in the face of death.

MOVING FORWARD OR MOVING ON?

I imagine the biblical Job as a proud father at his daughter's dance recital, clapping loudly, standing to take photos. You know the one; there's at least one in every auditorium! With a wife, seven strapping sons, and three beautiful daughters, Job's life seemed perfect. He loved with great intentionality, we are told; his family was his pride and joy. However, we hardly meet the dramatis personae in the book that bears his name when tragedy befalls Job. A windstorm blows through town and destroys his oldest son's home with all his children inside. Job is a man undone. He has endured what modern psychologists would call "catastrophic loss."

For the next forty-plus chapters, we watch Job wrestle with grief and the problems of evil and suffering in the world. We empathize with Job as he endures faithful friends who say all the wrong things. We raise our fists beside him as he argues with God. And as the story draws to a close, we stand in awe. God blesses Job's faithfulness with a brand-new family. Seven new sons and three new daughters—girls, we are told, who are the loveliest in the land. Full repayment for all he lost.

Or is it?

I've often wondered how Job's grief changed over those years. As he watched his seven new sons grow and thrive, as he bounced his new little girls on his knee, did he remember the children who used to shriek with glee as he tossed them play-fully in the air? As he taught his boys to care for the flocks, did his voice catch as he remembered guiding other little hands as they learned the day's chores? Even with all the joy God brought into his life after loss, could Job really move on? Surely he never forgot the children he had lost. The new family never replaced the old. No doubt, Job knew from experience, there was no moving on, only moving forward.

After the death of our loved one, we're often encouraged, "Someday you'll move on." If you're young, you might be encouraged to marry again. If you've lost a child, you're reminded, "You can have other children." Folks who love us long for linear progression and predictable signs of our improvement. They care about our well-being, even when they say such painfully untrue things. But moving on is something you do when you pick up and leave a campsite. It's not what you do when you leave a grave. Living after loss isn't like closing the chapter on a great novel and moving on to the sequel.

You won't ever forget the day the police officer arrived at your door, the day the doctors told you there was nothing more they could do. The image of the casket, the freshly dug grave— these are things you can't unsee. And neither should you want to. Our connection with our loved ones includes these painful moments as well as all the happy ones that preceded them.

Throughout Scripture, we see remembrance as a vital part of

community and personal identity. The cycle of Old Testament feasts not only reminded God's people of their past struggles, it also asked them to enact them. Seven times a year, the Israelites would stop to recall their slavery in Egypt, the toil of the harvest, the cost of their sin, and their longing for Messiah. There was no moving on from memories of their pain. Instead, connecting with the hard stories of their past was the key to wisdom, the pathway to moving forward.

The same goes for us as we learn to live with grief when it's no longer new. As the years pass, we need not close the door to memories. Instead, as we allow grief to do its work in us, we will discover that our love for our deceased person offers us the energy, inspiration, and hope to move forward. The stories of love and of pain that shaped us in the past are indispensable to our future.

WILL I EVER SMILE AGAIN?

Have you stood at the bathroom mirror and wondered if you'd ever smile again? After your world crumbles, the sorrow weighs so heavily that it's hard to imagine being able to ever really love life again. Grief blindsides us in public places, and sorrow so rearranges our lives that they are hardly recognizable anymore. It's easy and natural in the depths of grief to talk in superlatives—*never* and *always*—to describe the way we feel.

We often create a false dichotomy that grief is an all-or-nothing game, that we are either happy or sad, that our lives are marked by either joy or sorrow. When the intensity of those first days naturally fades, we fear this means that we love our person less. When crying ebbs, we're vexed. Do we miss them less? Have we replaced them?

If you have lost your sister, another living sibling will never replace her. If your husband has died, a remarriage won't supplant his place in your life. *You can't replace people.* Neither, it must be confessed, can you replace the life you lived before. Job's new children couldn't replace those he lost. Your new life after your person dies will never replace what you lived before. If we're to construct new lives after loss, we must release this all-or-nothing thinking. It's a lie as old as the Garden of Eden.

Run straight to Genesis 3, and you'll hear the serpent tell Eve the same all-or-nothing kind of lie. The lie that good things are withheld from you. The lie that God's plan is marked by scarcity, not abundance. At its core, "you'll never smile again" tells you those same untruths. It speaks the lie that happiness, like the sun in northern climates, is a limited resource. That God may allow tragedy, but he never redeems it.

Mark Henricks, a father whose son died by suicide, shared, "I don't expect ever to forget Brady, or ever to not care about what happened. But I do expect to someday learn to cope with his loss, to accept that he is gone, to be able to remember him fondly and to feel genuine happiness again in spite of everything that's happened. I think that is a reasonable expectation."

Mark is right. A smile, a laugh, true joy—they are all reasonable expectations after loss. In fact, if you want them, you can bank on finding them. We can smile again after loss if we choose to. We can laugh, we can love, we can find purpose. Why are these things possible, even probable? Because an almighty God calls us his beloved. God wrote resilience into our very DNA when he formed us out of dust. God designed a story where resurrection follows death. And, in those moments when grief

God wrote resilience into

our very DNA when he

formed us out of dust.

God designed a story where

resurrection follows death.

and sin and sorrow feel at their deepest, he remembers these things about us—that we are weak and made of dust, that his love for us commits him to our good.

Grief may linger as a lifelong companion, but as you become accustomed to its presence, you can be sure you'll smile again. You will smile again because God smiles on you. Even when you question his purposes. Even when you rail against his silence. Even when you weep for the one you've lost. You remain his beloved. His face is always toward you.

How do you get to this thriving life? Let's figure it out together.

IS IT OKAY TO KEEP GRIEVING?

When is grief no longer new? Is it after the first anniversary of your person's death? After a major life step forward like remarriage? How long is it okay to keep grieving? As I talk to grieving people, these questions of time frequent our conversations.

As you might have guessed by now, there's no single right answer. Your grief is no longer new when it's no longer new *to you*. You get to choose. Perhaps you feel more companionable with grief when the acute physical and emotional toll fades. Maybe you sense a shift as you pass the first set of holidays without your person. It could be an instant of change, but for most people, new life creeps in quietly. One day you realize you don't cry as much as you once did. One day you discover memories bring less piercing pain and more bittersweetness or even just a smile. I trust that, as you continually bring your sorrows before God and engage your suffering with intention, you'll know.

When Rob and I were first married, we used to have heated

discussions and sometimes sharp disagreements. In the normal course of welding two lives together, sometimes sparks flew. But over the years, we settled into an intimate companionship where we discovered we rarely disagreed. Gone were the debates. We'd grown to see eye to eye on big world topics and household matters. Even the significant additions of moves, job changes, and child-rearing caused relatively little rise in temperature. Our marriage was one of easy companionship, mutual trust, and deep understanding.

As I look back, there wasn't a single moment that caused that shift. Rather, the daily iron sharpening iron wore away many of our rough spots and lessened friction. Of course, we never became perfect. I remember well—and sadly—spats we endured. But as the years passed, our relationship became marked less by conflict and more by companionship.

I'm convinced grief's companionship can evolve in similar ways. The emotional, physical, and spiritual sparks that fly in the early, acute months and years of sorrow can shift into deep understanding of life's fragility, honest reckoning with our own mortality, and enthusiastic love for the life that still stretches out before us.

In the Old Testament, periods of mourning or outward manifestations of grief were marked by ritual. The community donned sackcloth and ashes to acknowledge mortality; men shaved their heads to embody their loss. Immediate burial was common in the ancient Near East, and Israel paused to mourn brothers Moses and Aaron for thirty days after their interment. When Jacob died, his son Joseph mourned for seven days beside the Jordan River. The Egyptians who had embalmed him set

Beth reflects on her father's death:

The sharp edges of grief have softened over time. The once intense and sudden waves of sorrow have grown infrequent, and I no longer notice the pain hourly or even daily. However, I still miss my dad's physical presence in this world, particularly in mine. A consummate educator, he gave many intangible gifts, but the very last one was my first real experience in grief.

Though unwanted, grief has been a good teacher. My father's premature death forced me to ask hard questions that ultimately deepened my faith in God, showed me the power of community, and opened my heart to the pain of others. And death taught me lament. I camped out in the book of Psalms and in the words of Nicholas Wolterstorff: "Every lament is a love-song."

Over the past decade much new life has come into my own—marriage, children, school, and life in an unfamiliar part of the country. But I can share none of this with my dad, and all my husband and daughters know of him are fragments from stories and pictures. I wish it were different—that he were still present in body, alive and active—yet his story lives on in me. Like his dynamic presence, his sudden absence shaped my identity for the better.

aside seventy days to publicly grieve. All these external practices informed the Jewish custom of sitting shiva, a mourning ritual that still exists today.

In a beautiful acknowledgment of the persistence of sorrow, Jewish tradition offers another ritual to grieving families. Annually, families mark their loved one's death through the celebration of Yahrzeit. This memorial occurs in perpetuity after a close family member dies, a reminder that there is no end to the remembrance of sorrow. At a Yahrzeit observance, families light a special long-burning candle, read psalms about the light of God, share stories, and give gifts in memory of their person. Yahrzeit holds space for the grief that remains. Even better, it integrates grief into new life by placing sorrow and suffering in the context of a God who delights in bringing light into darkness.

INTEGRATING YOUR GRIEF

The requirements of parenting after Rob's death have constantly pushed me forward, but you don't need the pressure of raising young children to compel you along after loss. If you've acknowledged that healing or recovery isn't the goal here, you can set your goal instead to integrate your loss as best you can. Before you think, *Another thing I need to do?* have no fear. Grief integration is what you've been working on this whole time! Since the first days of your loss, you've been facing death and learning to live with grief as your companion. You're doing it already!

Integrating grief simply means the slow acceptance of the changes in your life that come after the death of your person. You can make incremental adjustments to create new rhythms. As the years go by, you can grow in your understanding of your ability to stay bonded with your person even in their absence. Each day you press forward, you carry your loss into the life you now live without your person. And each day you carry your person into the life you now live without them.

Grief integration and companionship are lifelong relationship building tasks. Proverbs 14:13 reminds us that "even in laughter the heart may ache." J. William Worden of the Harvard Child Bereavement Study at Massachusetts General Hospital describes this lifelong work as a cycle of tasks that keep integrating your grief into your life as it grows around your loss. Worden writes that you cycle through acknowledging the reality of your loved one's death, feeling the pain of that absence, adjusting to life without your person, and finding ways to remain connected to them even as you move forward without them.

For the first year after Rob died, I'd wake up every morning and remember afresh that he was dead. At first, I lay each morning in bed and cried. After my tears were exhausted, I'd shuffle downstairs to set the water on to boil—a job he used to do. As I stood with a warm mug of tea in my hands, I'd remember his morning smell, his laugh, his warm arms around me. Sometimes the tears would flow again. In that simple daily ritual, I acknowledged the ache of Rob's absence and adjusted to life without him. I cried and heated the water myself. I recalled the intimacy of his body and plotted out my tasks for the day ahead as I drained my morning cup. I suspect you do similar rhythms of remembrance and integration every day.

By activating your desire for grief integration, you can move forward toward a life of flourishing after loss, even when it is hard. Learning and applying Worden's simple cycle can normalize the feelings of grief that persist after most people in your life think you should be "over it by now." Understanding your task of lifelong relationship building with grief, you can enact Worden's tasks regardless of the years that separate you from the death of your loved one.

Many years after my great-grandfather died, my father decided to compile his papers into book form. Great-Grampa Eduard, a Jewish convert to Christianity, had lived through World War II and fled to the United States with his family as refugees. I remember standing in the funeral home as a ten-year-old after his death in 1988. His was the first funeral I ever attended.

My father had long accepted his grandfather's death; but, years later, as he read through the journals and letters left behind, fresh grief sprang up. "There are so many things I wish I could ask him," he told me. Even after all that time, he mourned the loss of this beloved man. Now a grandfather himself, Dad brought a new perspective to his relationship with his own grandfather. In this new season, he needed to acknowledge, again, his grandfather's absence.

As it turned out, compiling that book offered my father beautiful ways to connect with his grandfather. The bond was not broken by death, only changed. All the love still existed, and Dad came to appreciate and celebrate his grandfather's investment in his life in new ways as he leafed through old pictures, transcribed journal entries, and engaged in genealogical research. Worden's four tasks of grieving intuitively offered him rich ways to process his loss in a new season and maintain connection to someone he still loved dearly.

LOVE LIVES ON

Acknowledging grief as a long-term companion invites you to continue the bond of love you held with the person you lost. If our goals are grief integration and a flourishing life after loss, we need to know from the very beginning that love lives on. This isn't Hallmark sentimentality; it's emotional reality. The love you held as you stood at your person's grave doesn't fade as the years go by. This is a gift in grief.

Three years now since Rob's death, I can't help but smile as I think of all the ways his love has released me to live again. Rob's death awakened in me gifts he always saw I had, and each time I engage these gifts, I feel a sense of his pleasure. I continue to love him as I see the investment he made in my life and in our children's lives. I tap into his wisdom as I use my own voice and mind to make decisions. I smile as I wrap myself in his favorite flannel shirt on a cold morning and remember that his love still keeps me warm, even if his arms never will again.

George Bonanno writes, "[Resilient people] know their loved one is gone, but when they think and talk about the deceased, they find that they haven't lost everything. The *relationship* is not completely gone. They can still call to mind and find joy in the positive shared experiences. It is as if some part of the relationship is still alive." C. S. Lewis describes this dawning in a similar way as he reflects on the death of his wife, Joy, in *A Grief Observed*. Nicholas Wolterstorff says as much in *Lament for a Son*. Over and over we discover that our loved one is actually part of that joy that emerges after death. The love that lives on empowers us to look ahead with hope.

What might this look like for you as the years go by? Nicole, who lost her husband when her children were little, created a "remembering room" in her new home to offer her children a quiet space filled with photo albums and their daddy's special items. Lynn turned her husband's old clothes into a quilt that keeps her cozy in bed each night. Jon and Kristen started a nonprofit inspired by their son's death. Kayla wrote a book. All of these—and more—constructively and creatively sought to continue their bonds of love, acknowledging the grief that lasts and inviting that grief to inform, clarify, and inspire their lives today.

Whether you wear your child's fingerprint on a necklace, memorialize your father with a brick at the local arboretum, or pursue that master's degree she always encouraged you to try, you can carry your person forward with you into your new life. For the most part, how we grieve over time is determined by "what we do with our memories, how we experience them, and what we take from them during bereavement." So whether you take up your person's hobby or simply allow their better qualities to inspire growth in your life, the love that lives on can invite growth into this new life you're creating.

LESS THAN HAPPY MEMORIES

The loss of a loved one doesn't always bring wistfulness. For many of us, the death of our person prompts many unhappy memories. Whether grief provokes memories of abuse, neglect, or alienation, or simply regret for unresolved disagreements, continuing the bonds of love can be complicated.

If abuse or neglect is part of your story, I encourage you to talk with a counselor or therapist to process the challenging emotions related to your loss. Moving forward in love may mean releasing unfulfilled or hurtful loves and stepping out in self-love toward your new future. The death of loved ones always brings complexity, even in the healthiest relationships. If yours has been a hard relationship, you deserve support and encouragement even as the years go by. It's never too late to ask for help.

In grief, you may find yourself wanting to rewrite the past. Sorrow may give you a view, for the first time, of your own sins. As a hedge against our own regrets, we often try to simplify complexities and smooth over our own wrongdoing. Death offers us no do-overs, and this can feel scary. What could be more dangerous, then, than to look into *that* rearview mirror with honesty?

The pathway to peace begins with honesty and confession. We don't reckon with the past by ignoring it. We discover peace in grief and relief from regret when we bring the truth into the light.

However, the pathway to peace begins with honesty and confession. We don't reckon with the past by ignoring it. We discover peace in grief and relief from regret when we bring the truth into the light. You can stop pretending the past was perfect and acknowledge that relationships weren't always what you had hoped, that the choices you made weren't always right. Continuing your bonds of love may mean first stopping to say, "I'm sorry."

The Grief Recovery Handbook offers a helpful exercise in apologizing and offering forgiveness to our deceased loved one in a way that can move us forward toward health. Authors John James and Russell Friedman encourage you to write a letter to your loved one in which you complete these three sentences:

- "I apologize for . . ."
- "I forgive you for . . ."
- "I want you to know . . ."

We all want to bring our person forward into the years ahead, but to do this without continual regret, we need to pursue inner peace. As we confess our sins to God, we can find resolution and restoration for the errors of our past, even when the person is no longer with us. We can find peace, even when we can't undo or redo. You can confess your sins in a letter to your person, silently to God, or to a trusted friend. You can make things right *now* so that grief's companionship need not add extra burden through the years to come.

A NEW OLD RING

A year after Rob died, as I was preparing my home to sell, I patched the backyard concrete patio. Weeks later, I noticed concrete had dried inside the prongs on my engagement ring. The diamond was cloudy and gray. My ring was ruined. Not long after that, I was assembling our kitchen table in our new rental when I crushed my anniversary band. I had to pry it open to get it off. Diamonds skittered across the kitchen floor. Two rings ruined in about a month.

I took my rings downtown to a jeweler who happened to be a widower. As he inspected the damage, we talked about how hard the decision was to wear or remove our rings. He shared what he'd done after his wife died, about the negative responses he'd gotten from people when he removed his ring and about how he'd had to learn to be okay with that part of moving forward. I felt a kinship immediately; this man understood how heavy this all was.

My rings were beyond repair, he said gently and honestly. But we could make something new of them. "That would become a family heirloom," he told me as he described his idea. I left my two rings in his safekeeping, and I talked to Rob aloud the whole way home. "He's going to make me an heirloom, honey," I told him. "It's going to be a ring that tells our story." I cried, got nervous, got excited, and cried again.

A month later, I went to pick up the beauty I now wear on my right hand. Two rings melted into a new one, seventeen tiny stones for the seventeen years of our marriage, and as its center-piece, the diamond Rob gave me twenty-one years ago when he proposed. "What do you think?" the jeweler asked as I turned the ring slowly under the light. I had no words; it was perfect. This precious widower had created a celebration of my marriage, a ring that will always tell the story of Rob and me—beauty out of sadness, honor always for the love that was and still remains.

Someday your grief will no longer be new. You'll discover you've accepted the reality of your loved one's death and started taking steps forward into a new life. You'll remember moments together with joy and draw strength and inspiration from them. You'll move toward flourishing because grief was never meant to break you but to remake you. As you integrate your grief into your new life, I hope you'll find—to your surprise, perhaps—that your person lives on in many ways. In your habits, your faith, your talents, and your interests. Grief, this expression of love when the object is gone, can become the catalyst for growth.

FOR YOUR OWN REFLECTION

1. Have you felt like you need to "move on" from your loved one's death? Have you been told you need to do it? What do you assume this means?

2. Do you feel like your grief has changed over time? If so, how? As you reflect on this, how does this change make you feel?

3. Think of a time when you've laughed or smiled since your person died. Did you try to feel good, or did you find that joy bubbled up on its own inside of you? How can joy coexist with suffering in your life?

4. Are some memories of your person hard to face? What can you do to explore and release some of these less than happy memories?

5. How can you continue your bond of love with your person who has died? What practical, everyday ways can you exhibit that love?

CHAPTER 10

Letting Grief Come to Church: Developing a Culture of Death and Resurrection

Oh, bless'd communion, fellowship divine!
We feebly struggle, they in glory shine,
yet all are one in thee, for all are thine.
Alleluia, alleluia!

WILLIAM WALSHAM HOW, "FOR ALL THE SAINTS"

In 2020, I nervously hit the "send" button on an article I'd written for *Christianity Today* about letting grief come to church. In that piece, I'd admitted something I hadn't been able to voice out loud to many people since Rob died: going to church after loss was hard. Harder than hard. Even though I'd called myself a follower of Jesus for most of my life, after my traumatic loss, church felt like the last place I could return.

For months after Rob's death, I wrestled with what to do. Sundays had always been uplifting—Sabbath after a busy week, an hour to recenter myself on what was important. In the years before death cast a shadow over my life, I would have described worship as satisfying, inspiring, and probing. But after what I'd endured, none of that was what I needed anymore.

I believed fully that God was sovereign, almighty, and all-knowing. But few moments in church life offered me the kind of Jesus I now longed for in my darkest hour—a fully human, wounded, broken, dying friend. Like the writer of Ecclesiastes, I reasoned, "It is better to go to a house of mourning than to go to a house of feasting, for death is the destiny of everyone." Church had always been for me a house of feasting. Now, its menu made me queasy. Perhaps, after Rob's death, I just didn't belong anymore. Maybe church just wasn't for me anymore.

I want to be clear that our local church community was kind and generous. They delivered delicious meals and donated generously to our children's education fund. Church members made repairs to our home and volunteered to help with yard work. And if we could have stayed at home forever, perhaps that would have been enough. But something intangible happened each time we attempted to cross the threshold of the sanctuary at church. We visited a variety of area churches, and the same thing occurred each time. Of all the spheres in which we interacted, church felt like the one place to which it was impossible to return. Of all the places where we had once belonged, church felt most foreign.

Author and widow Miriam Neff estimates that approximately 50 percent of widows leave the church they attended as a couple and lose 75 percent of their social network after their spouse dies. There are myriad reasons a person might leave a church following loss, such as lack of emotional or material support. But we had received that in abundance. Why did we feel like such strangers in a place that had once felt like home?

A few months after Rob died, I logged into an online grievers forum and searched for posts asking the question I felt I could not ask my local congregation. I needed to know I wasn't alone. Did anybody else feel like they couldn't go to church anymore?

The words I found amazed me. Among the faithful, as well as those whose religious affiliation was admittedly thin, the answer was the same. *I can't go back.* The woman who had watched her son suffer from terminal illness could eventually get her yearly mammogram done in the same hospital where he had died. The man whose wife loved sailing eventually took to the water again. But darkening the doors of the church felt daunting, nearly impossible, to many. A man shared his struggle of reintegrating into small group ministry where groups were divided into singles and married. (Where would a widower fit?) A woman talked about sitting in the back pew and crying through worship, convinced she'd never return again. I breathed a sigh of relief and then quickly held my breath. What would this mean for my spiritual life going forward? Why couldn't I return to this place I'd once loved? If the church was meant to be a hospital for the wounded, why did my brokenness seem not to fit?

After talking with pastors and lay leaders and grieving people all across the country, I'm convinced it doesn't need to be this way. Dear reader, the church needs your wounds. Your local congregation may not realize it yet, but it needs the wisdom birthed by all that you have endured. Even if you can't yet darken the doors of the sanctuary, I want to assure you: you still belong.

So, too, you need the church. Christianity isn't a lone wolf religion. Even if you've found peace for the spiritual questions you've carried after loss, you can't find flourishing outside the body of Christ. Life with Jesus was never meant to work that way.

If the death of your loved one has made you feel orphaned, I want you to know that I understand. I've wrestled with feelings of alienation and abandonment, disappointment and disillusion. However, you don't need to throw the baby out with the bathwater. In fact, I think as a grieving person you are uniquely a blessing to the church. In these days and months and even years when you may feel least equipped, God is gently forming beauty from your ashes, preparing you for gifts of love and service.

GRIEVING AND THE CHURCH

"Grieving well is best done within a supportive community that is willing to suffer, wait and care for the person devastated by a loss, and who in many ways is a new person," Rob wrote in *The Art of Dying.* "It is a tragedy that, for many, such a community doesn't exist." If the human experience of grief is one in which we can find connection, it is equally true that the spiritual dimensions of grief are best experienced in community. If we are honest, here the church has often woefully failed us.

It is no surprise that the church does not know what to do with grieving people. In corporate settings like Sunday worship, most churches function like a classroom teacher aiming for the middle, with little attention to those on the margins. Churches market positive, uplifting services and energetic, engaging weekend worship experiences. A church near my home claims, "We believe that kids should have a blast at church every single week." But what if the only energy you possess is sapped lifting your body from bed each day? What if your children experience a blast of grief every single morning when they rise and realize their father is gone?

Though we all bear burdens of grief (related or unrelated to death), the church often doesn't know what to do with those of us who have suffered loss. Our churches, built around family programming, hold little space for young parents who have lost a child, for husbands who have lost a wife. If the unspoken messages of the church are to be made plain, those needs are best met in individual care ministries. Few ministries are grief-aware enough to be prepared to engage with bereaved people who enter their regular programming. They, too, don't want to talk about death.

Rob wrote *The Art of Dying* because he wasn't satisfied with this status quo. As a hospice volunteer, he saw dying people who desperately needed community. As a funeral home employee, he interacted with mourning families who needed a spiritual anchor in the rough seas of acute grief. He saw hurting people like you and me, and his call in *The Art of Dying* was clear: we must do this better.

Since I began writing on grief after Rob's death, there are many times I've thought, *Honey, you were right.* Any husband would be thrilled to hear his wife say that, wouldn't he? But it's true. Over and over I have seen that by preparing to die, we learn to live well; by facing death, we acknowledge the hope of Christ. At the risk of sounding like a broken record, I say nothing new. In the most beautiful way possible, I stand on my dear husband's words.

However, I'm a person who learns by doing. I struggle to

conceptualize without the opportunity to put an idea into action. As I connect with you on social media and in person, I know you need action too. You needed a church ready to care for you *yesterday*. Before your hope and stamina fades, you need to know you still belong, that there's a place for you, that the church can become all that you—and a hurting world—so desperately need.

Good news: I'm convinced you and I don't need to wait any longer. Jesus stands with open arms, inviting us into worship and service. We may be wounded, but we are still members of his body. We can build the church we need. Our presence in worship and service reminds the church of its central mission. To borrow the words of Teresa of Avila, "Yours are the eyes through which Christ's compassion for the world is to look out . . . and yours are the hands with which He is to bless us now."

HOSPITALITY BEGINS WITH "HOSPITAL"

For the first half of my career, I worked in the nonprofit world. I advocated for refugees and fair trade organizations. I told the stories of small-town baseball leagues and orphans with special needs. A common thread wove through everywhere I worked: those who felt called to serve others had once been the recipients of care. Ministry leaders who had personally known the sting of rejection opened their hearts to the marginalized. Nonprofit leaders recalled the stories of those who had inspired their work—those who had cheered them on when they were unsure and loved them when they felt unnoticed. Out of their pain, their passions and purpose grew.

Dear reader, this is true for you, too. Grief does not

disqualify you from ministry or involvement in the church. You don't need to be healed to help, to be courageous to contribute. There is a place for you in the church—always. You are always welcome. Hospitality begins with "hospital." Welcome always includes care.

As you walk with grief, no doubt you've discovered gifts born of this difficult relationship. If you allow it, grief develops within you new capacities for care and service, a heightened sensitivity and tenderness toward the needs of others. Like the widows in 1 Timothy, your loss has qualified you for ministry in ways you never could have developed on a résumé.

Furthermore, grief deepens your theology of suffering and glory. Your heart is more attuned toward heaven. The old gospel hymn rings true: "I've never been this homesick before." C. S. Lewis notes that "our life as Christians begins by being baptised into a death; our most joyous festivals begin with, and centre upon, the broken body and the shed blood. . . . Our joy has to be the sort of joy which can coexist with that." You have lived this reality; its truth is now written on your heart.

In a tragic but beautiful way, your loss has equipped you to bless the church. Your very presence in the sanctuary, in the Sunday school classroom, or on the work team reminds those around you that Jesus does not call the healthy but the sick into his care. And those he calls, he empowers and equips to do his gracious will. More important, your presence as a grieving person reminds the church that the Christian story finds its roots not in bold triumph but in selfless woundedness. Just as you belong in church, a wounded Jesus does too.

One of the greatest gifts of my grief experience has

been meeting Jesus as fully human—afraid in the garden of Gethsemane, wounded by those who hated him, dying for those he loved. Over and over I have discovered Jesus in Scripture as a vulnerable person just like me. His self-emptying has astounded me and drawn me near. "He is one who has been over every inch of the road," writes Elisabeth Elliot, words echoed in the old Puritan hymn. "Christ leads me through no darker rooms than He went through before."

In a church culture often infected with worldly triumphalism, we need regular reminders that the risen Christ we worship bears real, human scars. He is not an esoteric high priest but an earthly Holy God. Our presence in church reminds us and the whole congregation that we need to welcome the wounded Jesus back to church. We need him in our sanctuaries to offer balanced, thoughtful worship. We need him in our ministries to remind us of our purpose.

"Christianity teaches us that the terrible task [death] has already in some sense been accomplished for us," Lewis writes. "That a master's hand is holding ours as we attempt to trace the difficult letters and that our script need only be a 'copy,' not an original." What a glorious relief these words are! We can let grief come to church without fear. We can reshape the church's culture to reflect both death and resurrection. All of this is possible because Jesus has done the hard work for us already.

THE HOME YOU NEED

"The kingdom of heaven is like . . ." When I read those words in the Gospels, I imagine the crowds that followed Jesus. Unfolding their lawn chairs, they shushed their children and leaned in to

Grief care is not a niche

ministry because death is not

a niche experience. Instead,

grief ministry is regular,

whole-church ministry.

hear better over the quiet crackling of unwrapping lunches. For centuries, Israel longed for God's good Kingdom to come. The prophets' promises were written on their hearts. It's no wonder that when Jesus said those words, a hush fell over the crowd. It was time to dream. No, better than that. It was time to visualize a real future, so close you could almost touch it.

When we talk about reshaping church culture to reflect both death and resurrection, we're not talking about a pie-in-the-sky impossibility. We're not talking about a dream for the future. We're simply inviting our local congregations to be what Jesus has always called us to be—a real vision of the inbreaking of God's good Kingdom in the here and now. The church home grieving people need isn't different from the church we have now. It is simply *more* of the church we have now.

Grief care is not a niche ministry because death is not a niche experience. Instead, grief ministry is regular, whole-church ministry. Paul tells the Corinthian church that the church's ministry of comfort flows from the comfort we receive from God. Again, he tells the Philippian church that the consolation we know in Christ overflows into care for one another. The function of the church is marvelously simple: know Christ and make him known. How do we do this for hurting people? We offer the comfort—spiritual, emotional, material—we have ourselves received. A congregation marked by death and resurrection simply needs to lean more fully into the mission Jesus has assigned each of us to do.

Right now, in this season of your life, you need a church home with a specific kind of grief-awareness. You need a congregation whose heart is formed with empathy and understanding toward physical death. But here's the thing. That knowledge isn't experience-specific. As our churches become more formed into cultures of death and resurrection, we'll discover we're more equipped to offer comfort in myriad ways.

I often like to say that if every grieving person wore black to church, every single person in the sanctuary would be wearing black. We all have something hard we're carrying, a loss we're feeling—whether it's fresh and searing or an old, dull ache. If you'd worried a grief-aware church was catering only to people like you, have no fear. We are a world of grieving people; each one needs what Jesus has to offer. I'm convinced envisioning and building toward the church we need will bless every single person who crosses your sanctuary's threshold.

GRIEF CARE, GRIEF AWARE

"What we say about death and resurrection gives shape and color to everything else," writes N. T. Wright. What master-piece could God shape your faith community to be as you invite grief to come to church? Put on your creative cap, and let's imagine for a moment what that would look like in your local congregation. Imagine what it would be like for grief to make its home in church in the same way it has made companionship in your life.

First, grief would be welcome in worship. We know that right away, don't we? Lament would become a regular, normal form of worship, not only reserved for Advent Blue Sundays or Good Friday services. Through music, prayer, and the Word, we could engage weekly with a risen Jesus who still wears his scars, whose woundedness is the gateway to intimate communion with him.

Jeremy reflects on pastoring the grieving:

When I left my last pastorate, our church sent us out with a box full of letters. One letter was from a young lady who had been suffering from debilitating depression and self-harm related to loss.

She wrote, "My friend urged me to attend your church. I agreed, but I had already made up my mind that after the service I was going to end my life. I was hopeless and hurting and I figured the church wasn't a place for people like me. But then, when the service began, you welcomed people with a poem that said the very opposite of what I thought about the church. God met me that day, and I left with hope for the first time."

The poem she was referring to is something I penned to welcome people into our church community. I wanted the variety of human experience to be recognized and greeted right away. People are often coming to church tired, discouraged, and suffering in some way. They need this welcome:

To the broken and in need, to the lonely and afraid,
To the weary who are looking for hope in the midst of pain,
To the skeptic with many doubts, to the strong in faith and growing,
To the stranger in our midst and the one whose heart is hurting,
Here you find a church of the forgiven and undeserving.

Our worship would include the full narrative arc of Scripture, inviting those who rejoice to grieve with those who mourn and those who mourn to be carried forward on the praise of those who rejoice. We would offer space for the wide range of emotions our encounters with God produce. We would acknowledge with passion, sorrow, and hope that we live in the messy middle of a story that is yet to know its culmination. We would pray with longing, "Your Kingdom come." We would regularly encounter Jesus' death at the Communion table and weekly confess our common hope: *We believe in the communion of saints, the resurrection of the dead, and the life of the world to come.* We would offer our grief to be transformed by the glory that we know awaits us.

As people of the Living Word, we would invite grief to transform our spiritual formation, too. If death and resurrection shape all we do, we would educate ourselves in the rich history of Christian death and dying. We would turn to saints past and present for instruction on how to live faithfully in our last days. Grief awareness would permeate every classroom and hallway in our ministry centers. Children would learn about Jesus' death without teachers fearing a depressing lesson. Teens would see how our mortality must frame our engagement with the world. Adults would learn to measure their days to gain hearts of wisdom. Grief could sit comfortably, knowing that lesson plans infused hope into the very real ways that brokenness marks our days.

Finally, grief's presence in our churches would radically reorient the way we care for one another in suffering. Niche ministries like meal trains and handyman work teams would overflow with volunteers who understood that what hurting people need isn't perfection but presence. We would become fluent in words of consolation, knowing what to say and when to say it because we regularly interfaced with death and dying. We would know each other's needs in loss because grief made regular appearances in our sanctuaries, classrooms, and ministry teams. We would intentionally work to integrate grieving members into church life, trusting that the fullness of Christ could fill all in all, even when loss remains.

THE THREE SONGS OF THE CHURCH

Young Isaac Watts sat in church and let his mind drift away from the music around him. From birth his parents had brought him each Lord's Day to the Congregational Church in Southampton, a nonconformist gathering of Puritans along the English coast. Each week, the congregation sang simple melodies, slowly working their way through the book of Psalms. Isaac knew the words by heart.

Though he acknowledged the words as holy writ, Isaac longed for words that spoke his heart language. He sensed from the dull intonation of others around him that they did too. He longed for worship to reflect the wide range of experiences believers faced as they walked with Christ. Challenged by his deacon father to "write something better," Isaac set to work.

The following week, Watts presented his first hymn—"Behold the Glories of the Lamb"—to the enthusiastic praise of his local congregation. They requested another and another and another. Soon, Watts's new career path was clear. Over the next fifty years of his life, he would pen over seven hundred more hymns, earning the names "Poet of the Sanctuary" and "Father of English Hymnody." While singing extrabiblical words initially made some of his Puritan friends uneasy, Watts's words and melodies would establish themselves at the core of Christian worship music for generations to come. We can thank Isaac Watts for "Joy to the World," "Our God, Our Help in Ages Past," and "When I Survey the Wondrous Cross," among many others.

What was it that struck a chord for those who listened to Watts's words those many years ago? What had young Isaac drawn from Scripture to fall fresh on the hearts of those who gathered in worship? Had he really, as his first hymn says, "[Prepared] new honors for His name, and songs before unknown"? I suspect not. Instead, Isaac Watts helped congregations rediscover the three songs the church has always sung and will always sing until Jesus comes again. Watts had tuned believers' voices for laud and lament and longing.

When we look at the rhythm of the Christian life, these three melodies weave together to create our collective song. We laud, praising God for his sovereignty, power, and love. We lament, acknowledging our individual and corporate sinfulness and the brokenness of the world. And we long, lifting our eyes toward the promises of Christ's return and God's renewal of all creation. All other songs are caught up in these three great melodies. No church can sing the full song of gospel truth without them.

As we consider the church we long for in grief, we must acknowledge the necessity of each of these three songs. Each one is deeply needed to offer space for our broken humanity and for the extravagant hope we possess in Jesus. Grieving people need space to lament in worship and church life; we need time and room to plumb the depths of loss and sorrow.

> *The church must anchor us in the truths of God's steadfast goodness when life's storms threaten to overwhelm us. The church must act as a lighthouse, shining God's love and grace when death and grief make all around feel dark.*

But we also need to laud. The church must anchor us in the truths of God's steadfast goodness when life's storms threaten to drown us. The church must act as a lighthouse, shining God's love and grace when death and grief make all around feel dark.

And if we are to find hope and flourishing again after loss, the church must help us long. Not with nostalgia for what was but with fervent hope for what will be. If death is to be swallowed up in victory, we must ever have our eyes lifted, directed beyond the cross to the empty tomb.

Mixed among Isaac Watts's most famous hymns stand a few that might catch your eye. "Death! 'Tis a Melancholy Day" probably won't become the next worship music chart topper, but Watts's words picture so well how comfort and hope can rise when we allow the church to sing its three best songs:

> *See how the pit gapes wide for you,*
> *And flashes in your face!*
> *And thou, my soul, look downwards too,*
> *And sing recovering grace.*

When we invite grief to church, we discover a fuller gospel that enlivens us, even when we must stand at the freshly dug grave of the one we love. When the pit gapes wide, we can still sing our songs of recovering grace. When tears fill our eyes, we can still lift our hearts in prayer and praise.

LIVING WITH LAMENT

For our family, the three years since Rob's death have been a season of deep lament. Only eight months after his death, grief's shadow widened as the COVID-19 pandemic spread around the world. Social and political unrest revealed the depth of this world's darkness. One tragedy after another brought a relentless stream of lament into our lives. If ever I felt "fast falls the eventide," it was then.

During that season, a single prayer emerged that has echoed a faithful refrain within the sanctuary of my heart. In our year of solitary quiet in quarantine. Amid the shouts and weeping of televised protests. Each night as I lie in my bed alone after turning out the lights. Into the darkness of those days and into these, through tears and in hoarse whispers, I have pleaded, "Come quickly, Lord Jesus."

Life has taught me the bitter song of lament. I have cried out to God in anger, frustration, and sorrow. On particularly dark days, I have asked, "My God, my God, why have you forsaken me?" I have wept by the rivers of exile when I remembered the good life I left behind when I began to walk a widow's path. The weight of grief's presence in my life has often felt more than I could bear. My prayers echo the distressed cries of C. S. Lewis's sweet young Lucy: "Aslan, Aslan, if ever you loved us at all, send us help now."

Since Rob died, lament has been my sorrowful tune, yet beneath the melody has run the steady harmony of longing, the sweet refrain of praise. Its faithful beat has surprised me more than once. I've come to believe the Christian cannot have one without the other. To lament without longing is simply to despair. To long without lament is wishful thinking. To long and lament without laud is to miss the joy of Christ altogether.

I began this chapter telling you that the church needs you,

that your grief is a gift to your congregation. I hope you can better see why. Brokenness is always the pathway to the gospel. Jesus' wounds will always be our source of comfort and healing. Even in your deepest pain, you belong to the church. Together, we'll sing our songs of laud, lament, and longing until Jesus comes again.

FOR YOUR OWN REFLECTION

1. After your person died, what was your experience with your church community? What practical, emotional, or spiritual support did they offer?

2. Do you feel like your woundedness doesn't fit in church? If not, why not? What would you need to feel welcome there?

3. Lament feels natural in grief, but laud may not. What is the place of praise in the grieving person's life?

4. How does being with your congregation increase your longing for your person? For God's good Kingdom? How does this increased longing make you feel?

5. How can your grief offer you insight into ministry that you didn't have before? How can grief be an asset, not a liability, in your service?

CHAPTER 11

Journey's End: Lifting Our Eyes, Longing for Home

Our Father refreshes us on the journey with some pleasant inns,
but will not encourage us to mistake them for home.

C. S. LEWIS, *THE PROBLEM OF PAIN*

On one of our favorite family hikes in Washington's Cascade Mountains, there's a turn in the trail that always gives me pause. After almost two miles of walking through towering western red cedars and Douglas firs, a space opens up on the northerly side of the trail. For the first time, your gaze can rise beyond the trail at your feet to the expanse beyond. Through a frame of trees, the sky expands and you see verdant, forested mountains, layer after layer on to the horizon.

Whenever we get to this spot on the trail, I insist on a stop. A rocky ledge juts out between the trees, and I climb over, take a seat, and catch my breath—only to have it taken away again. The slog of the trail feels so different up here, high above the rest of the world, surrounded by mountain majesty. If the most beautiful views are found at the hardest climbs, I daresay, this trail is worth every footfall.

The old gospel hymn assures us, "It will be worth it all when we see Jesus. Life's trials will seem so small when we see Christ." But when you're in the slough of grief, truth is often obscured by the muck and mire of sorrow. It might even feel cliché. When your eyes are so trained on the rocky, rooted trail before you, it can be hard to hear that you need to lift your eyes to look for more.

If life doesn't shine quite as brightly anymore or our days feel emptier, it's not because death has taken away our joy. It is because death has revealed to us a greater longing—for a joy that lasts, unbroken, abounding, forever and ever.

But for the believer, no book about grief can simply be about emotion management or behavior modification. The tools of doctors and psychologists are good gifts of God to his people, but the hope that lights our way in grief shines beyond all that human effort can ever achieve. Our hope in life and death will always be, as the Heidelberg Catechism says, that we belong to Christ. Because of his death and resurrection, the assurance of eternal life with him empowers us to be "heartily willing and ready" to live our allotted days for him.

For believers, the hope of the gospel shapes our grief. It is the lens through which we view death. It colors our sorrow and infuses our sadness with persistent joy. It reminds us that the flourishing we pursue in this life is only a foretaste of all that is to come. Hope, for the Christian, is everything.

The seventeenth-century theologian François Fénelon wrote, "We can hope only to the extent that we are dissatisfied with the world." Dear reader, he's talking to you and me. In the loss of our loved ones, we have experienced our own dissatisfaction with the world. If life doesn't shine quite as brightly anymore or our days feel emptier, it's not because death has taken away our joy. It is because death has revealed to us a greater longing—for a joy that lasts, unbroken, abounding, forever and ever. In the face of death, we can hope with ever more fervor because we see clearly what we may never have seen before. Perhaps, for the first time, we are lifting our eyes and longing for home.

N. T. Wright tells us, "God's plan is not to abandon this world, the world which he said was 'very good.' Rather, he intends to remake it. And when he does, he will raise all his people to new *bodily* life to live in it. That is the promise of the Christian gospel." This is the truth in which we stand. Moreover, it is the truth we are living into each day. The power that raised Jesus Christ from the dead is accessible to us now through his Spirit. The new life that awaits us has already begun. As Romans 13:11 says, "Salvation is nearer now than when we first believed."

Because this truth enlivens us, we can be assured that flourishing awaits those of us who grieve, not just in the future but here and now. Just as our redemption began the first moment we believed, our new life after loss has already begun. It is our calling, then, to step forward and take hold of it with passion and purpose. With grief as our companion, we can live with joy as we eagerly await the fulfillment of God's promises, knowing that the inauguration of his good and peaceable kingdom has already begun. Our feet are already pointed toward home.

A joyful, deeply satisfying life awaits you after loss.

Take a deep, cleansing breath, and read that sentence again: *A joyful, deeply satisfying life awaits you after loss.*

Like God's anointing word at Creation, he calls your life good. The hope he offers is more than just hanging on. It is breath and energy and purpose and joy. And, most glorious, this life stands waiting for you. Yes, *you*. Not the heroic ones or the scrappy, tenacious ones. You—just as you are in your brokenness, in your sorrow, in the rubble of the life you knew before. *A joyful, deeply satisfying life awaits you after loss.*

How do I know this? I see it on the hikes I take with my children, and I read it in God's Word. God has built all of creation for resilience, and resurrection is always his gracious pleasure.

DESIGNED FOR RESILIENCE

After my boys arrive home from their baseball games, they're ravenous. They'll plow through a bag of tortilla chips or a whole box of cereal if I let them. It makes sense. Their growing bodies have just expended lots of energy. They need to replenish and restore. Since I know that proteins and sugars hasten muscle recovery after exercise, I try to slip a peanut butter banana in front of them as they chow down.

With the right care and rest, muscles broken down grow stronger. Wounded skin scabs and heals. If you've been a smoker and quit, even your lung tissue can repair. Rob wrote about brain plasticity in his second book, *What Your Body*

Knows about God, and I spent many dinner hours listening with fascination as he talked about how prayer and meditative practices could literally rewire our brains. Resilience is built into every cell of our bodies. God designed you marvelously to physically recover from difficulty. When I say, "You will get through this"—the sleepless nights, the stomach upsets, the physical exhaustion—I'm not selling you snake oil. God made you to recover.

God has built us for emotional resilience as well. Just as your body can repair from the physical stress of grief, your heart can also repair from the emotional toll of acute sorrow. I want to be clear here that when I talk about "repair," I'm not saying you'll be healed, that you won't feel the pain of your loss anymore, that you'll bounce back and be a bigger, better you. Instead, I like to think of the repairing work of emotional resilience as a broadening perspective shift. God has designed each of us for emotional resilience, regardless of whether we'd call ourselves optimists or pessimists. We can use the tools he gives us to reshape our perspective after loss and build a new, beautiful life with grief as our companion. God has wired us with the capacity to learn and grow, to allow our experiences to broaden and deepen our wisdom.

Almost two decades ago, Dr. Toni Bisconti published a landmark study at the University of Akron in which she defined "dispositional resilience," a repairing perspective that she had observed could help bereaved people discover flourishing after loss. Her contemporary, George Bonanno, had already determined that personality predicted "only about 10% of resilience," and Bisconti wanted to know what made up the other

90 percent. In the study, Bisconti outlined five qualities an emotionally resilient person could develop:

- Connectedness
- Mastery
- Inquisitiveness
- Hardiness
- Flexibility

What did a person need to survive and thrive again after loss? She needed a supportive community where she could strengthen old relationships and build new ones. She needed to feel like her grief was manageable, that she could wrap her head around what had happened to her. To become emotionally resilient, she'd need to be willing to try new things, being open to failure as well as success. Finally, she'd need to stick with it, persistently living—sometimes one day at a time and other times taking big leaps into the new life that lay before her.

Do you know what I find most magnificent about this list? These are things *any of us* can do. Resilience after loss doesn't depend on financial resources or education or career status (although these things can be helpful). It isn't more likely with women but less likely with men. Resilience doesn't discriminate if you've lost your child in an accident or your spouse from dementia. God's marvelous, innate design of our bodies and spirits to repair and recover is accessible to each one of us.

If you've heard the condolence response, "I could never be that strong," go ahead and politely stop the person midsentence. Nothing could be further from the truth. With God's design for our bodies working together with the power of his Spirit within us, our weakness can become strength. Or, as the prophet Isaiah says it, "The LORD will guide you always; he will satisfy your needs in a sun-scorched land and will strengthen your frame. You will be like a well-watered garden, like a spring whose waters never fail." We can flourish again.

So how do we work with this great gift of resilience God offers us in our bodies? I love how Elisabeth Elliot describes a fellow widow's resilience: "She prayed and she did the next thing. She picked up the broom."

As comforter and guide, the Holy Spirit supports you as you engage in the rebuilding work that God has laid before you. Therefore, you can seek out mentors to help you chart your new course. You can rely on your faith community to support you in practical, emotional, and spiritual ways as you re-form your identity after loss. You can practice dispositional resilience just like you practice repairing your body after exercise. And you can trust that the Holy Spirit will strengthen you with his power to look forward with hope.

GROWING AGAIN

Growing again after loss, even when you know we're built for resilience, can bring a lot of unsolicited advice. You might even second-guess whether you want it. Since your person died, have you heard the encouragement, "He would want you to . . ."? *He would want you to take that trip. She would want you to marry again. He would want you to be happy.* It can be hard to feel like we must consult our dead person about our decisions in the now.

Post-loss growth is about more than maintaining your

connection with your loved one. You're already doing that regularly. Post-loss growth is your choice to harness your resilience to grow, to release the impulse to stagnate.

To some extent, you will always see your life as BD/AD—before death and after death. That's what a dramatic event like death does. Our whole system of numbering years is based on Jesus' death as its pivot point! But pursuing post-loss growth means that we resist the urge to rank the past as more valuable than the present or force ourselves to see the future as the most valuable of all. We can simply receive this moment and ask how we can use it best.

Growth after loss happens when we make the clear shift from wishing to doing. When we move from *I want to see change* to *I need to make it happen.* As we discover the new parts in us that grief has birthed, we choose to celebrate them. We notice increasing capacities. We make small, everyday choices to, in the words of author Ann Patchett, "choose a life that will keep expanding."

Though it can initially seem daunting, post-loss growth is easily within your grasp. A good place to start is to ask yourself the question, *What do I want?* Beyond having your person back, think macro and micro. What places in your life do you want to see expand? What skills do you want to learn? How do you mobilize the wisdom you've gained from grief for good?

It's okay to be resistant to identity growth. This isn't a year-long task but an emerging endeavor. As you step forward into your new life, expect a normal oscillation between grief and growth. Remember that the waves feel most intense at the beginning. The oscillation between grief and growth will move more slowly and gently with time. George Bonanno calls these beginning steps toward growth "coping ugly." Holding tightly to God's promise of resilience, you can move forward toward building a life you love even if it doesn't look pretty at the beginning. Taking a new job, renovating your home, beginning a nonprofit in memory of your person, dating again—all of these growth activities begin with small, faltering steps. Internal growth of expanded introspection works just the same way. As you're rebuilding and coping ugly, remember C. S. Lewis's encouragement: "We are, not metaphorically but in very truth, a Divine work of art, something that God is making." You're a masterpiece in progress.

BUILT FOR RESILIENCE, MADE FOR RESURRECTION

Eight months after Rob died, my friend Melissa stood in my living room writing on Post-it notes and sticking them to a bare window. I couldn't figure out what parts of me (if any) had survived his death, and together we were working to name them. I'd run on fumes for the better part of a year—solo parenting by the seat of my pants, lost in a sea of death-related paperwork. I was trying to rebuild my life but terrified to step forward into a future where Rob would never be present. I longed for the old me; I needed reminding she was still there. I needed clarity.

That night, I determined to pull parts of me out of the rubble of my traumatic loss and make them live again. I thought that's all life after loss was about—resuscitating what remained. I didn't realize resurrection meant more than just bringing dead things alive again. I had no idea I could have a life I loved again. But three years later, I find that I do. Because resurrection isn't just the reversal of death. It's the good made even better. Resurrection is *all things made new*. This is the life God offers us after loss—not only a resilient life but a resurrected one.

There's not a day that I don't miss Rob. Sometimes the ache still takes away my breath. But even in those most painful moments, I celebrate resurrection. I claim it as my own. We may be built for resilience, but through grief I have learned this truth: resurrection is always God's gracious work alone. I cannot awaken what is dead. Only God can do that. Furthermore, because of Jesus' resurrection, our eternal hope isn't just for heaven or the new creation in the future. When that tomb emptied on Easter Sunday, our eternal hope began. We do not only wait for resurrection life. Even in the midst of grief, we can live it now.

FROM DEATH, LIFE

"Did you know babies have webbed hands in the womb?" my daughter asks me on the ride home from school. She's taking Honors Biology and has become a DNA and genetics junkie. "How come they're not born with their hands that way?" I ask, happy for a new topic to draw conversation out of my usually quiet eldest. As though she's just been waiting for me to ask, my daughter launches into a full discussion of the marvels of apoptosis, programmed cell death. I listen and marvel. Death is everywhere. It's even in our cells before we're born.

As it turns out, apoptosis is a vital process for all living things. In apoptosis, cells destruct and die to give way for new cell life. This systematic, regulated process of dying actually makes our

Each day is worth facing
because a risen Jesus offers
you not only resilience
after loss but grave-defying
restoration. You can love
life after loss.

bodies live. It's a vital mechanism for healthy physical growth. Humans experience billions of cell deaths in their bodies each day; parts of us are dying all the time. Tadpoles lose their tails and become frogs thanks to apoptosis. Precancerous cells are destroyed by the body thanks to apoptosis. We count our newborns' ten tiny, individual toes thanks to apoptosis.

It's hard to believe that any death can be good or useful. But in the case of apoptosis, death isn't just good or useful; it's necessary. Without this highly controlled process, cancer cells grow and birth defects develop. The body sentences some cells to death for a larger purpose: healthy new cells.

As I listen to my daughter, I marvel at how much these phenomena sound like Jesus' words in the Gospels: "I tell you the truth, unless a kernel of wheat is planted in the soil and dies, it remains alone. But its death will produce many new kernels— a plentiful harvest of new lives." Death always precedes new life.

I recognize this story arc of death and resurrection. I am living it every day. Rob's death has prompted a sort of elemental death in me. The old cells of our life together are breaking down. Though much of the process is slow and smaller than my eyes can easily see, I know that his death is effecting big changes in me. I may look the same on the outside, but I am becoming different down to my very cells.

Through the power of the Holy Spirit, we have access not just to a future hope but to a powerful living hope. Each day we live with grief, we can access "his incomparably great power," says the apostle Paul to the Ephesians. The same power that raised Jesus Christ from the dead can raise you from the dead too. If you've felt like a part of you died after your person's death, I hope this comes as amazingly good news. God delights to make dead things alive again. He can and will do it for you, too.

What will resurrection life look like for you in the here and now? I'm not sure. Your experience will be as unique as mine. I don't know the specific ways God will make you alive again. I don't know how your life's shape will change as you step into the resurrection hope he offers you each day. We each have the choice of how our person's death changes us. Will your encounter with loss produce life again? Will you allow your loved one's death to reorient your priorities, your relationships, your calling, your faith?

However it works for you, I firmly believe that if you claim this resurrection hope as your own, you will see the intricate beauties of new life unfold in your life. The resurrection promises of God will bear fruit in your own life. You will watch your mourning shift to dancing. You will pack up the sackcloth one day and dress instead in the new clothing of joy. You will learn to claim your new name—"Oak of Righteousness"—a tree planted by streams of water whose roots have not withered even in the most trying circumstances. Your flourishing will truly be "the planting of the LORD, that he may be glorified."

Our loved one's death transforms us in the very hardest ways and in beautiful ways too. Parts of you died with your person's death, parts survived, and—amazingly—parts have been born. Each day is worth facing because a risen Jesus offers you not only resilience after loss but grave-defying restoration.

You can love life after loss. In grief and joy, God offers you a life made new, full to overflowing with his goodness.

Even with this resurrection power running through our veins, life isn't easy. Will life after loss become perfect, uncomplicated, or linear? Not this side of glory. But that's the wonder of it all. The resurrection life we can enjoy today, in the midst of sorrow, is just a foretaste. As new life grows inside us after loss, we experience the firstfruits of the great joy that awaits us.

COMING HOME

Sometimes in a quiet moment, I imagine what it will be like to see Rob again. At night, I've dreamed of him, but they're all nightmares—him leaving over and over again. I take comfort to remember that what awaits us someday is more glorious than any dream I could ever dream anyway. Even as I pursue a life marked by resilience and growth, even as I claim resurrection as a mercy for each new morning, I long for something more. I find myself more than ever lifting my eyes and longing for home.

For the Christian, the journey of grief has an end. One day soon, grief will no longer cast a shadow on our path. This unwelcome companion is a temporary comrade on the journey. One day we will know the culmination of resurrection. *So too shall we be with the Lord.* Together with our loved ones we will enjoy what N. T. Wright calls "the life after life after death." One day, we will feast in the house of Zion. "All the things that have ever deeply possessed your soul have been but hints of it—tantalising glimpses, promises never quite fulfilled, echoes that died away just as they caught your ear," imagines Lewis.

If your journey with grief shifts anything within you, I hope it increases your longing for glory a hundredfold. Our lives, so often rooted in the here and now, need a reorienting toward eternity, not as a way of escaping the hard places we find ourselves in but as a way of contextualizing and redeeming them. Jesus told his disciples, "Now is your time of grief, but I will see you again and you will rejoice, and no one will take away your joy." I cling to that promise, and I hope you do too. One day, no one will take away your joy—not even death. The old order of things will have passed away.

In deep grief, it may be hard to grasp this as more than an esoteric truth. That's why I've found it helpful to think specifically of Rob's face. I imagine him as part of the great cloud of witnesses cheering me on. He stands beside my grandparents and his, beside my friend's mother, and near a fellow widow's husband. He rubs shoulders with your loved one; they exchange hugs of greeting. They know fully even as they are known. The crowd is bustling with an energy that could only be described as holy excitement. Salvation is nearer than when any of us first believed. The communion of saints waits in anticipation for the trumpet to sound, for the New Jerusalem to descend as a bride prepared for her husband. You can almost hear the crowd begin to shout Isaiah's ancient words:

> Surely this is our God;
> we trusted in him, and he saved us.
> This is the LORD, we trusted in him;
> let us rejoice and be glad in his salvation.

ISAIAH 25:9

AIN'T NO GRAVE

We began our journey together at the graveside of my loved one and yours. That day you heard the first handful of soil fall on the casket, you began your walk with grief, the hardest path you've ever endured. Grief's companionship has shaped you, teaching you the full weight of sorrow and strengthening you for the life that lies ahead. You have pointed your feet toward flourishing with your Shepherd walking close at hand.

We are admonished by the apostle Paul to grieve as those who believe the gospel. We are called to sing with tear-stained eyes the words that our Black brothers and sisters sang in tenacious hope: "In that great gettin' up mornin', ain't no grave gonna hold my body down." It feels appropriate, then, to end our walk together at another grave, this one an empty tomb.

When I talk to grieving Christians, they'll often tell me, "I don't know how someone could do this without Jesus." And I have to agree. The empty tomb does not negate the graves we stand beside in this life, but it does transform them. As Paul reminds the Thessalonians, "We believe that Jesus died and rose again, and so we believe that God will bring with Jesus those who have fallen asleep in him."

In the end, we can embrace grief's companionship because of the empty tomb. When we're aching and exhausted, the empty tomb reminds us that transformed bodies await us. When we feel the piercing loneliness of sorrow, the empty tomb assures us that death will lose its sting. For the Christian, the empty tomb is the hinge pin of our hope in grief. Resurrection awaits those we love, and it awaits us, too. And though at times you'll find it hard to believe, this hardest path you've ever walked will lead you home.

FOR YOUR OWN REFLECTION

1. How does it make you feel to know that God designed you for resilience?

2. Look back at Dr. Toni Bisconti's marks of dispositional resilience (see page 202). How can you develop in these areas of your life?

3. What growth have you already seen in your life since your person's death?

4. What might resurrection look like for you today? Where are you seeing dead things come alive again, transformed and brand new?

5. Do you long for the new creation? In what practical ways can you increase that longing in your life as you wait for Jesus' return?

ACKNOWLEDGMENTS

I owe a special debt of gratitude to these dear ones who have walked with me through grief toward flourishing, from the conception of this book to its birth.

David Horn, thank you for telling me to write and giving me a point to walk toward in early grief. Al Hsu and Sarah Zylstra, thank you for your love for Rob that has overflowed in enthusiastic encouragement of my work. Jason and Jaylynn Byassee, Collin Hansen, and Madison and Regina Trammel, I'm so glad God's goodness has woven our lives together for so many years. Thank you for your wisdom and generous support as I crafted these words. Sara Billups and Ann Voskamp, thank you for encouraging me to write in the midst of vulnerability. Jenny Chapman, thank you for your friendship in sorrow. Liz Cumming, you introduced me to grief's companionship; thank you for walking with me toward hope.

Books are made like cars, a million little parts put together by a host of talented hands. This book is no different. Thank you,

Ann Kroeker, for encouraging me to write a list of ten ideas when I thought I had no more. Thank you, Gina Henker, for providing editing and feedback on my early drafts. Melissa Zaldivar, your companionship in the publishing trenches can't be beat. Andrew Wolgemuth, Jillian Schlossberg, and Jonathan Schindler, thank you for your wise and gentle shepherding of these pages. Daniel Harrell and Mike Cosper, thank you for inviting me to explore in our "Surprised by Grief" podcast many of the thoughts developed here. I am grateful for our friendship. Thank you to all those who shared their stories of grief and hope to enrich these pages.

Though it has often seemed to the contrary, this book's creation has only been a sliver of my life. In this season of grief and growth, I have found a life richly supported by the love and kindness of so many. My deepest gratitude to my World Vision family and my church families in Seattle and Massachusetts for supporting me in the steepest learning curve of my life. Alisa, Amanda, Beth, Cindy, Joyce, Julia, Kathy, Kelsey, Kristy, and Marissa, thank you for belonging to me in love. Aaron, Adam, Chris, David, Jeremiah, and Todd, thank you for the texts and tips and fishing trips; your love is rebuilding us. Jill and Brian, thank you for walking with us through darkness toward the light. To my family near and far, my gratitude will always feel inadequate to the enormity of your love and care. Thank you.

Finally, to the ones who have lived every word with me. Kids, *we made it*. Your lives sing the most beautiful resurrection song. Thank you for cheering me on, for sharing the Internet bandwidth, and for making my life rich and full. Let's celebrate with whoopie pies.

And to Rob, these words are because of you in all the very best and hardest ways. I love you. I miss you. Words fail, beloved. Words will ever fail.

NOTES

Introduction

xiii   *"The LORD is close to the brokenhearted"*: Psalm 34:18.

Chapter 1: On the Path with Sorrow and Suffering: The Journey Nobody Wants to Take

3   *"I can't go with them . . . It is more than I can bear"*: Hannah Hurnard, *Hinds' Feet on High Places: An Engaging Visual Journey* (Carol Stream, IL: Tyndale, 2017), 27.

4   *"I shall not die, but live, and declare the works of the Lord"*: See Psalm 118:17.

14   *"Others have gone this way before me . . . and they could even sing about it afterwards"*: Hannah Hurnard, *Hinds' Feet on High Places: An Engaging Visual Journey* (Carol Stream, IL: Tyndale, 2017), 28.

Chapter 2: Obstacles on the Path: Four Myths We Believe about Grief and Loss

26   *eighteenth-century colonial Puritans . . . parades through the streets*: Steven C. Bullock, "'Often Concerned in Funerals': Ritual, Material Culture, and the Large Funeral in the Age of Samuel Sewall," in *New Views of New England: Studies in Material and Visual Culture, 1680–1830*, ed. Martha J. McNamara and Georgia B. Barnhill (Boston: Colonial Society of Massachusetts, 2012), 198.

26   Puritans "even prayed that their grief would 'never wear off '": David
      Hackett Fischer, *Albion's Seed: Four British Folkways in America*
      (New York: Oxford University Press, 1989), 114.

28   "endurance produces character, and character produces hope":
      Romans 5:4, ESV.

28   "our present sufferings . . . the glory that will be revealed in us":
      Romans 8:18.

28   Multiple research studies . . . result in resilience and life satisfaction:
      M. D. Seery, E. A. Holman, and R. C. Silver, "Whatever Does
      Not Kill Us: Cumulative Lifetime Adversity, Vulnerability, and
      Resilience," *Journal of Personality and Social Psychology* 99, no. 6
      (December 2010): 1025–41, https://doi.org/10.1037/a0021344.

Chapter 3: Meeting Grief: Getting to Know Your New Companion

38   Isaiah 53 tells us that Jesus would be "acquainted" with grief: Isaiah
      53:3, ESV.

50   It seemed as though . . . joy and pleasure at the same time: Hannah
      Hurnard, *Hinds' Feet on High Places: An Engaging Visual Journey*
      (Carol Stream, IL: Tyndale, 2017), 71.

Chapter 4: Aching Bones and Sleepless Nights: Physical Dimensions of Loss

62   "If anyone hears my voice . . . eat with him, and he with me":
      Revelation 3:20, ESV.

63   "Sadness dampens our biological systems . . . seems to slow the world
      down": George A. Bonanno, *The Other Side of Sadness: What the
      New Science of Bereavement Tells Us about Life after Loss* (New York:
      Basic Books, 2009), 32.

63   In fact, Bonanno says, sadness . . . adaptation after loss: Bonanno,
      The Other Side of Sadness, 31.

68   "We live and move and have our being": Acts 17:28, ESV, emphasis
      added.

69   I dreaded the visit and almost canceled a couple of times because of
      cold feet: Visit https://clarissamoll.files.wordpress.com/2021/03
      /goingtothedoctor.pdf for "5 Tips: Going to the Doctor after
      Loss."

72   "We had our hopes up that he was . . . the One about to deliver
      Israel": Luke 24:21, MSG.

74   "Stay and have supper with us. It's nearly evening; the day is done":
      Luke 24:29, MSG.

Chapter 5: Bushwhacking through the Forest: Navigating the Practical Dimensions of Loss

Chapter 6: On the Shores of Loneliness: Wading through the Emotions of Loss

Chapter 7: Dark Nights beneath the Stars: Searching for Spiritual Answers to Loss

126   *"The LORD has brought me back empty"*: Ruth 1:21.

127   *"The Almighty has brought misfortune upon me"*: Ruth 1:21.

127   *"A broken spirit, a broken heart . . . all you have to offer"*: Elliot, *Suffering Is Never for Nothing*, 80.

128   *"Lament is the language . . . trust in those promises through the tears"*: Mark Vroegop, *Dark Clouds, Deep Mercy: Discovering the Grace of Lament* (Wheaton, IL: Crossway, 2019), 44.

130   *"Why do you hide yourself in times of trouble?"*: Psalm 10:1.

130   *"People are meant to live . . . being spoken to"*: Dallas Willard, *Hearing God: Developing a Conversational Relationship with God* (Downers Grove, IL: IVP Books, 2012), 20.

130   *"The LORD's hand has turned against me"*: Ruth 1:13.

133   *"[The LORD] has not stopped showing his kindness . . . to the living and the dead"*: Ruth 2:20.

133   *"No matter how well . . . Jesus was not spared"*: Dallas Willard, *Hearing God through the Year: A 365-Day Devotional*, comp. and ed. Jan Johnson (Downers Grove, IL: InterVarsity Press, 2004), 321.

134   *"Naomi has a son!"*: Ruth 4:17.

Chapter 8: And a Little Child Shall Lead Them: Parenting through Loss

139   *Research estimates that approximately one in fourteen . . . lose a sibling during childhood*: "Childhood Bereavement Estimation Model," Judi's House/JAG Institute, accessed October 28, 2021, https://judishouse.org/research-tools/cbem/.

140   *Children who suffered loss became presidents or prisoners*: Twelve US presidents lost fathers as children, and prison inmates are "two to three times more likely to have lost a parent in childhood." Robert Krulwich, "Successful Children Who Lost a Parent— Why Are There So Many of Them?" NPR, October 16, 2013, https://www.npr.org/sections/krulwich/2013/10/15/234737083 /successful-children-who-lost-a-parent-why-are-there-so-many -of-them.

144   *"as children grow, they will need . . . each stage of development"*: Brook Noel and Pamela D. Blair, *I Wasn't Ready to Say Goodbye: Surviving, Coping and Healing after the Sudden Death of a Loved One* (Naperville, IL: Sourcebooks, 2008), 102.

148   *"bereaved children do not experience continual . . . behavioral*

grief reactions": Noel and Blair, *I Wasn't Ready to Say Goodbye*, 101.

Chapter 9: The Trail Ahead: When Grief Is No Longer New

164   *"I don't expect ever to forget Brady . . . a reasonable expectation"*: Mark Henricks, "Do You Really Never Get Over Losing a Child?," *Grieve Well* (blog), August 12, 2017, https://grievewellblog.wordpress .com/2017/08/12/do-you-really-never-get-over-losing-a-child/.

170   *William Worden . . . even as you move forward without them*: Marcia L. Howland, "Worden's Tasks of Mourning: A Spiritual Exercise," Crossroads Hospice Charitable Foundation, July 22, 2016, https://crhcf.org/insights/wordens-tasks-of-mourning -spiritual-exercise/#:~:text=Worden%20identifies%20four %20tasks%20in,reality%20of%20a%20new%20life.

172   *"[Resilient people] know their loved one is gone . . . some part of the relationship is still alive"*: George A. Bonanno, *The Other Side of Sadness: What the New Science of Bereavement Tells Us about Life after Loss* (New York: Basic Books, 2009), 73.

173   *"what we do with our memories . . . what we take from them during bereavement"*: Bonanno, *The Other Side of Sadness*, 71.

174   The Grief Recovery Handbook . . . *"I want you to know . . ."*: John W. James and Russell Friedman, *The Grief Recovery Handbook: The Action Program for Moving beyond Death, Divorce, and Other Losses Including Health, Career, and Faith* (New York: Collins Living, 2009), 145–51.

Chapter 10: Letting Grief Come to Church: Developing a Culture of Death and Resurrection

180   *"It is better to go to a house of mourning . . . for death is the destiny of everyone"*: Ecclesiastes 7:2.

180   *Author and widow Miriam Neff estimates . . . social network after their spouse dies*: Miriam Neff, "The Widow's Might," *Christianity Today*, January 18, 2008, https://www.christianitytoday.com/ct /2008/january/26.42.html.

182   *"Grieving well is best done within a supportive community . . . for many, such a community doesn't exist"*: Rob Moll, with afterword by Clarissa Moll, *The Art of Dying* (Downers Grove, IL: InterVarsity Press, 2021), 130.

185   *Like the widows in 1 Timothy, your loss . . . never could have developed on a résumé*: Moll, *The Art of Dying*, 152.

185   *"Our life as Christians begins by being baptized . . . sort of joy which can coexist with that"*: C. S. Lewis, *Reflections on the Psalms* (New York: Harcourt, 1986), 52.

186   *"He is one who has been over every inch . . . darker rooms than He went through before"*: Elisabeth Elliot, *Suffering Is Never for Nothing* (Nashville: B & H, 2019), 30.

186   *"Christianity teaches us that the terrible task . . . need only be a 'copy,' not an original"*: C. S. Lewis, *The Problem of Pain* (New York: HarperOne, 2001), 103–4.

189   *"What we say about death and resurrection gives shape and color to everything else"*: N. T. Wright, *Surprised by Hope: Rethinking Heaven, the Resurrection, and the Mission of the Church* (New York: HarperOne, 2008), 25.

192   *Young Isaac Watts sat in church . . . Isaac set to work*: "Isaac Watts: Father of English Hymnody," *Christianity Today*, accessed October 14, 2021, https://www.christianitytoday.com/history/people/poets /isaac-watts.html.

195   *"Aslan, Aslan, if ever you loved us at all, send us help now"*: C. S. Lewis, *The Voyage of the* Dawn Treader (New York: HarperCollins, 1980), 202.

Chapter 11: Journey's End: Lifting Our Eyes, Longing for Home

199   *"We can hope only to the extent that we are dissatisfied with the world"*: François Fénelon, *The Complete Fénelon*, trans. and ed. Robert J. Edmonson and Hal M. Helms (Brewster, MA: Paraclete Press, 2008), 203.

199   *"God's plan is not to abandon this world . . . the promise of the Christian gospel"*: N. T. Wright, *Simply Christian: Why Christianity Makes Sense* (New York: HarperOne, 2006), 219.

202   *Almost two decades ago, Dr. Toni Bisconti . . . know what made up the other 90 percent*: Ruth Davis Konigsberg, *The Truth about Grief: The Myth of Its Five Stages and the New Science of Loss* (New York: Simon & Schuster, 2011),160–61.

202   *In the study . . . what had happened to her*: Konigsberg, *The Truth about Grief,* 160.

203   *"The LORD will guide you always . . . like a spring whose waters never fail"*: Isaiah 58:11.

203   *"She prayed and she did the next thing. She picked up the broom"*: Elisabeth Elliot, *Suffering Is Never for Nothing* (Nashville: B & H, 2019), 88.

203   *And you can trust that the Holy Spirit will strengthen . . . look forward with hope*: See Ephesians 3:16-20.

204   *"Choose a life that will keep expanding"*: Ann Patchett, *What Now?* (New York: HarperCollins, 2008), 77.

205   *George Bonanno calls these beginning steps toward growth "coping ugly"*: George Bonanno, *The Other Side of Sadness: What the New Science of Bereavement Tells Us about Life after Loss* (New York: Basic Books, 2009), 78.

205   *"We are, not metaphorically but in very truth, a Divine work of art, something that God is making"*: C. S. Lewis, *The Problem of Pain* (New York: HarperOne, 2001), 34.

208   *"I tell you the truth, unless a kernel of wheat . . . a plentiful harvest of new lives"*: John 12:24, NLT.

208   *"His incomparably great power"*: Ephesians 1:19.

209   *"Oak of Righteousness" . . . "the planting of the LORD, that he may be glorified"*: Isaiah 61:3, ESV.

210   *"The life after life after death"*: Wright, *Simply Christian*.

210   *"All the things that have ever deeply possessed . . . died away just as they caught your ear"*: Lewis, *The Problem of Pain*, 150–51.

211   *"Now is your time of grief . . . no one will take away your joy"*: John 16:22.

211   *The old order of things will have passed away*: See Revelation 21:4.

212   *"We believe that Jesus died and rose again . . . bring with Jesus those who have fallen asleep in him"*: 1 Thessalonians 4:14.

ABOUT THE AUTHOR

Clarissa Moll is an award-winning writer and podcaster who helps bereaved people find flourishing after loss.

Before the tragic death of her husband, Rob, in 2019, Clarissa worked in education and nonprofit communications in organizations across the denominational spectrum. She holds a bachelor's degree in communications from Cedarville University and a master's degree in church history and systematic theology from Trinity Evangelical Divinity School. Clarissa has taught on the adjunct faculties at Cedarville and Wheaton College. She also holds a graduate certificate in nonprofit management from the University of Texas at Austin.

Clarissa's writing has appeared in *Christianity Today*, The Gospel Coalition, *RELEVANT*, Modern Loss, *Grief Digest*, and more. She penned the afterword for her husband's book, *The Art of Dying* (InterVarsity Press), and her writing on forgiveness appeared in *Along the Way: Real Life Moments Touched by God*

(Meredith Books), an anthology of inspirational writing for young adults. In 2020, Clarissa received an award from the Evangelical Press Association for her writing at The Gospel Coalition.

Clarissa cohosts *Christianity Today*'s *Surprised by Grief* podcast and hosts *The Writerly Life* podcast produced by hope*writers, an online membership community that equips writers for the publishing journey. Clarissa is a frequent guest on podcasts and radio shows, where listeners appreciate her refreshing honesty about grief and her commitment to hope in the midst of sorrow.

Clarissa lives a joyful life with her four children and rescue pup. She calls both New England and the Pacific Northwest home. Find her on Instagram at @mollclarissa or at clarissamoll.com.